THE COMPLETE
ILLUSTRATED
GUIDEBOOK TO

PROSPECT
PARK
AND THE
BROOKLYN
BOTANIC
GARDEN

Concept, Design, Photography and Maps by
Richard J. Berenson

Text by Neil deMause

Produced for
Silver Lining Books
New York
by
Berenson Design & Books, Ltd.
New York

SILVER LINING BOOKS

NEW YORK

Copyright © 2001 by Silver Lining Books

All photographs copyright © 2001 by Richard J. Berenson,
   except as noted below

Prospect Park map copyright © 2001 Prospect Park Alliance
   Design and digital rendering by Richard J. Berenson

Brooklyn Botanic Garden map © 2001 by Richard J. Berenson

For information address:
Silver Lining Books, 122 Fifth Avenue, New York, NY 10011

Library of Congress Cataloging-in-Publication Data
is available on request.

ISBN 0-7607-2213-7

Second Printing

Additional credits copyright:

Brooklyn Botanic Garden: *142-143 top*
   Christine M. Douglas: *154 bottom*
   Helena Fierlinger: *120 top, 121 top and bottom, 155*
   Betsy Pinover: *120 bottom*
   Rodica Prato: *130-131*

Cornell University/Making of America Collection: *28 bottom*

Herbert Mitchell Collection: *55*

Library of Congress, Washington, DC: *22-23 top*
   Manuscript Division, Frederick Law Olmsted Papers: *25 bottom*

The Museum of the City of New York: *25 top, 27*

National Park Service, Frederick Law Olmsted
   National Historic Site: *40-41 top*

Prospect Park Alliance Archive: *66-67 bottom, 67 middle, 76, 78,*
   79 (E.E. Rutter Collection, 6/10/1928)

Annual Reports of the Department of Parks,
   Prospect Park Alliance Archive:
   23 middle, 1896; 28-29 top (1861-73);
   29 bottom, 30-31 (1894); 37 bottom (1897);
   39 top (1871); 40 bottom (1894); 44-45 bottom (1886);
   47 bottom (1890); 57 (1868); 59 (1897);
   60-61 top (1869); 72-73 top (1873); 74-75 (1897)

Wildlife Conservation Society: *88-90, 91 top*
   D. DeMello: *Snowy Owl, Parma Wallaby*
   B. Meng: *Tree Nymph Frog*
   E. Kellerman: *Cotten-topped Tamarin, Red Panda, Bald Eagle*
   D. Shapiro: *Capybara, Hamadryas Baboons, Meerkats, Emerald Boa*

The illustrations appearing on pages 94-97 are reproduced from
BOOK OF NORTH AMERICAN BIRDS,
copyright © 1990 The Reader's Digest Association, Inc.
Used by permission of The Reader's Digest Association, Inc.

*This book is dedicated to
Frederick Law Olmsted and Calvert Vaux
for their inspired vision
and to the staff and volunteers
of the
Prospect Park Alliance,
The Parks Department,
and the
Brooklyn Botanic Garden.*

Contents

PROSPECT PARK

How to Get There 6
A Short History of Brooklyn . . . 8
Maps of the Park 12
Tours of the Park 18
Enjoying the Park 20
Creation of the Park 22

Tour of Grand Army Plaza . . . 32
Soldier's and Sailor's
    Memorial Arch 32
Sidebar: Frederic MacMonnies . . 36
Bailey Fountain 37
Statues of Kennedy, Skene 37
Statues of Warren and Slocum . 38
Park Entrance 39
Meadowport Arch 39

Tour of Long Meadow 40
Picnic House and Sullivan Hill . 42
Tennis House 44
Upper and Lower Pool 46
Bandshell 49
Lafayette Monument 49
Litchfield Villa 50

Tour of the Ravine 50
Sidebar: Geology of the Park . . . 52
Fallkill 53
Upper Pool 54
Ambergill 55
Ambergill Falls 55
Rustic Shelter 56
Boulder Bridge 56

Tour of Long Meadow East . . . 57
Endale Arch 57
Vale of Cashmere 59
Rose Garden 59
Nellie's Lawn 60
Battle Pass and
    Site of the Dongan Oak 60
Nethermead 61
Sidebar: The Battle of Brooklyn . 62
Binnenwater 64
Music Pagoda 64
Lullwater 65
Boathouse 66
Lullwater Bridge 68
Camperdown Elm 69
Cleft Ridge Span 70
Terrace Bridge 70

Tour of the Lake 71
Concert Grove 71
Oriental Pavilion 71
Sculpture in the Concert Grove . 72
Statue of Lincoln 73
Wollman Rink 73
Sidebar: Music in the Park 74
The Lake 75
Wildlife on and in the Lake . . . 75
Boating on the Lake 76
Honor Roll Memorial 76

Drummers' Grove 76
Pergola and Peristyle 79
Horse Tamers 79
Parade Grounds 79
Wellhouse 80
Peninsula 81
Maryland Monument 81

Tour of Lookout and
    Quaker Hills 81
Lookout Hill 81
Quaker Hill 82

Willink Tour 83
Willink Entrance 83
Carousel 84
East Wood Arch 84
Flatbush Turnpike Tollbooth . . 84
Lefferts Homestead Children's
    Historic House Museum 85

Prospect Park Zoo 86
The World of Animals and
    Discovery Trail 90
Animal Lifestyles 90
Animals in Our Lives 91
Lioness Statue 91

Sports in the Park 92
Wildlife in the Park 94
Trees in the Park 98

PROSPECT PARK ZOO
MAP PAGE 86

MAP PAGES
16-17

PARK
CIRCLE

PERISTYLE

PARADE GROUNDS

LAK

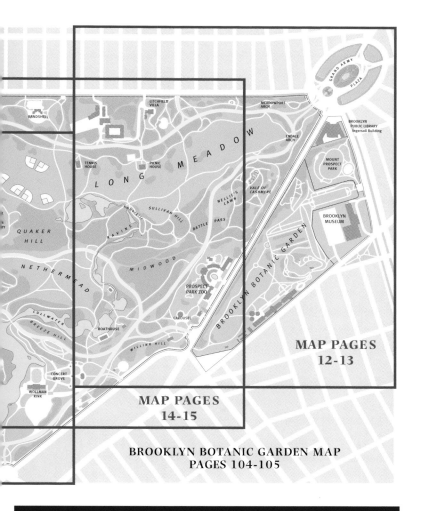

BROOKLYN BOTANIC GARDEN MAP
PAGES 104-105

BROOKLYN BOTANIC GARDEN

Enjoying the Garden 102
Map of the Garden 104
History of the Garden 107
Garden Entrances 108
Osborne Garden 108
Louisa Clark Spencer
   Lilac Collection 110
Rhododendrons 112
Native Flora Garden Tour 112
   Serpentine Rock 112
   Dry Meadow and Kettle Pond 112
   Bog 113
   Limestone Ledge 113
   Pine Barrens 113
   Wet Meadow 114
   Deciduous Woodland 114
Cranford Rose Garden 114
Cherry Walk & Esplanade 119
Sidebar: Sakura
   Matsuri Festival 120
Herb Garden 122
Shakespeare Garden 125
Fragrance Garden 127
Japanese Hill-and-Pond Garden 128
Sidebar: Tour of the Japanese
   Hill-and-Pond Garden 130

Celebrity Path 132
Magnolia Plaza 133
Plant Family Collection Tour . . . 134
   Conifers 134
   Ginkgo 136
   Beeches and Birches 138
   Bluebell Wood 138
   Elm and Pawpaw Trees 139
   Laurels and Roses 139
   Legumes and Citruses 139
   Heaths and Olives 140
   Monocot Border 141
Peony and Iris Garden 136
Rock Garden 142
Lily Pool Terrace 143
Steinhardt Conservatory 146
   Trail of Evolution 146
   C.V. Starr Bonsai Museum . . 147
   Robert W. Wilson
      Aquatic House 148
   Desert Pavilion 151
   Tropical Pavilion 151
   Helen Mattin
      Warm Temperate Pavilion .153
Children's Garden 155
Discovery Garden 155
   Index 156

HOW TO GET THERE

PROSPECT PARK

By Subway

For the Grand Army Plaza entrance, take the 2 or 3 trains to the Grand Army Plaza stop, then walk around or on the west side of the plaza to the park; for the Willink Entrance, take the D, Q, or Franklin Avenue Shuttle to the Prospect Park station on Flatbush Avenue or on Lincoln Road. The Parkside Avenue stop on the D/Q will take you to the Parkside and Ocean Avenue entrance. For travel to the west side of the park, take the F train to the 7th Avenue or Prospect Park stops and for the south end of the park use the Fort Hamilton Parkway stop.

By Bus

The park's north and west sides (Grand Army Plaza and the Long Meadow) can be reached by B41 or B71 along Flatbush Avenue to Grand Army Plaza, the B69 along Prospect Park West, or the B75 to the 9th St. entrance. The B68 travels to points along the southwest edge of Prospect Park, while the B12, B16, B41, B43, and B48 all take passengers to park entrances on the east side of the park.

By Car

From Manhattan, Prospect Park is best reached by taking the Manhattan Bridge, then following Flatbush Avenue to Grand Army Plaza. If you come via the Brooklyn Bridge, make the first left turn at the end of the bridge onto Tillary Street, turn right onto Flatbush Avenue and straight to Grand Army Plaza. Follow the circle around (Plaza Street West) to the right, then turn right onto Prospect Park West for parking.

From Staten Island or New Jersey, the park is accessible via the Verrazano Bridge and Brooklyn-Queens Expressway (BQE). Exit the BQE at the Prospect Expressway, take the 10th/11th Avenue exit, turn left, and drive four blocks to the park. Turn right and drive around Park Circle onto Parkside Avenue. Continue to Ocean Avenue. From points east, one can take the Belt Parkway or BQE to the Prospect Expressway, or follow Eastern Parkway to Grand Army Plaza.

It should be noted that for access onto the park's drives only the entrance at Parkside and Ocean avenues is open to cars during the majority of non-rush hour times.

Parking

Street parking is available but very limited. Visitors can park in the Litchfield Villa lot opposite 5th St. and, during business hours, at Wollman Rink. Parking is also available near the Brooklyn Botanic Garden (see below).

BROOKLYN BOTANIC GARDEN

By Subway

Take the D, Q, or Franklin Avenue Shuttle to the Prospect Park station or take the 2 or 3 trains to Eastern Parkway - Brooklyn Museum stop.

By Bus

B41, B43, B48, and B71. There are visitor entrances on Flatbush Avenue and Eastern Parkway.

By Car

From Manhattan, Brooklyn Botanic Garden is best reached by taking the Manhattan Bridge, then following Flatbush Avenue to Grand Army Plaza. If you come via the Brooklyn Bridge make the first left turn at the end of the bridge onto Tillary Street, turn right onto Flatbush Avenue and continue straight to Grand Army Plaza. Follow the circle two thirds around, then turn right onto Eastern Parkway (library on the right); go one block and turn right onto Washington Avenue (Brooklyn Museum on the corner).

From Staten Island or New Jersey, the garden is accessible via the Verrazano Bridge and Brooklyn-Queens Expressway (BQE). Exit the BQE at the Prospect Expressway, take the 10th/11th Avenue exit, turn left, and drive four blocks to the garden. From points east, one can take the Belt Parkway or BQE to the Prospect Expressway, or follow Eastern Parkway and turn south at Washington Avenue.

From Eastern Long Island, take the Jackie Robinson Parkway. Exit at Bushwick Avenue, turn left at third traffic light onto Eastern Parkway. Continue 3 miles and turn left onto Washington Avenue (The Brooklyn Museum is on the corner).

Parking

Street parking is available, or visitors can park at the Brooklyn Museum lot (for a fee) at 900 Washington Avenue.

A Short History of Brooklyn

Brooklyn is an oddity among American urban areas: Not officially a city, it is far more than a neighborhood. It is, in fact, a designation known as a "borough," one of the five regions New York City was divided into during the Consolidation of 1898, 31 years after the opening of Prospect Park. At the time of its assimilation, Brooklyn was the third-largest city in the country; today it would be fourth, having been surpassed by Los Angeles and Chicago in the intervening years.

Until the 17th century, Brooklyn was home to several thousand Lenape Indians (among them the Canarsie tribe), who lived in several villages scattered across what was then known as the southwestern section of Long Island. The Lenapes, or Delawares as they were renamed by the English settlers, harvested fruits and vegetables, fished and gathered shellfish in the Atlantic Ocean, and hunted wild animals that lived in the region's woods and marshes.

All that changed with the arrival in 1635 of the Dutch West India Company, which established settlements that would become today's Flatlands and Flatbush (the latter a corruption of the Dutch term "vlackebos," or wooden plain). They were soon joined by other villages of Dutch and English at New Utrecht, Bushwick, Gravesend, and an encampment on the heights overlooking Manhattan, which was dubbed Breuckelen, after a town in the Netherlands.

The Lenapes were soon driven out or killed by the English and Dutch settlers, and the farming settlements remained largely unchanged for the next 200 years, save for the forced importation of increasing numbers of African slaves to work the land. But Brooklyn, as the name became anglicized, became an important commercial town serving the rapidly growing New York City across the river. In 1816, two years after Robert Fulton's revolutionary steam ferry made commuting between Brooklyn and New York a possibility, the town was officially incorporated as the Village of Brooklyn; 18 years later, it became a city, with glazier and temperance advocate George Hall elected as its first mayor. (Hall is notable in that he served two terms as mayor of Brooklyn: the first in 1834, the second from 1855 to 1856.) As the new city grew, it swallowed up many of its surrounding towns, acquiring the city of Williamsburgh and the town of Bushwick to the north in 1854. By 1860, Brooklyn had more than a quarter-million residents, and was the nation's third-largest city behind New York and Philadelphia.

As the city grew, its leaders began to have dreams of competing with New York for both economic supremacy and grandeur of amenities. At the time, Brooklyn's only significant green space was Green-Wood Cemetery, which had been laid out in 1838 on high ground near the harbor front. Families would take excursions to the cemetery on Sundays, but it was no substitute for a genuine park.

City leaders, among them the prominent businessman and philanthropist James Stranahan, felt a grand park was necessary both to compete with Manhattan's new Central Park and to attract more affluent residents to the horsecar

The city of Brooklyn circa 1879. Prospect Park can be seen near the horizon at the upper right and an anticipation of the then unfinished Brooklyn Bridge at lower left.

suburbs then envisioned for the farmland that stretched between Brooklyn and the town of Flatbush. It was Stranahan who, as head of Brooklyn's parks commission, brought in Calvert Vaux and Frederick Law Olmsted, the designers of Central Park, to work their magic on a vacant, hilly parcel far from Brooklyn's downtown and turn it into the city's centerpiece. Stranahan's plan worked: By 1871, property values around Prospect Park had been raised by an estimated $77 million.

The creation of Prospect Park was not the only way in which Olmsted and Vaux transformed the development of Brooklyn. The partners also laid out plans to link Brooklyn's far-flung communities via a series of "parkways"—then a term for a landscaped boulevard, not the euphemism for highway that it would later become. Two were ultimately built: Eastern Parkway, which runs from Grand Army Plaza at the park's northern corner east through Crown Heights and Ocean Hill-Brownsville; and Ocean Parkway, which starts at Park Circle at the park's southern tip and runs all the way to Coney Island. To this day, the two avenues still comprise distinct neighborhoods

miles long and just a couple hundred feet wide, with stately shade trees and promenades that bring a taste of parkland to the city streets.

The next step in Brooklyn's development as a city was the creation of the Brooklyn Bridge in 1883. At the behest of *Brooklyn Eagle* publisher and Democratic party boss William Kingsley a bill was shepherded through the state legislature authorizing the bridge's construction. (Kingsley, who had overseen much of the contruction work on Prospect Park, would eventually become the bridge's chief contractor.) The bridge that gave Brooklyn its worldwide fame also helped lead to its downfall as an independent city. With Brooklyn and New York physically linked, many leading politicians and businessmen, including Stranahan, began lobbying for the two cities to be joined politically as well. Although many Brooklynites opposed the consolidation, in 1898, Manhattan, Brooklyn, The Bronx, Queens, and Staten Island were merged into Greater New York, under a single municipal government. Brooklyn would henceforth be just one of the city's five boroughs—but one that would forever retain its character as "America's fourth largest city."

PROSPECT PARK

Tennis House

Friends or Quaker Cemetery (Private)

QUAKER HILL

Fallkill Pool
Upper Pool
Fallkill Falls
Fallkill Bridge

CENTER DRIVE

NETHERMEAD

LOOKOUT HILL

Maryland Monument

Wellhouse

WELLHOUSE DRIVE

LULLWATER

Terrace Bridge

BREEZE HILL

PENINSULA

LAKE

Mozart

Oriental Pavilion

Wollman Rink

Beethoven

Lincoln

Moore

Grieg

Weber

Rustic Shelter

Honor Roll Monument

CARRIAGE CONCOURSE (Parking)

Imagination Playground

Rustic Shelter

DUCK ISLAND

Rustic Shelter

EAST LAKE DRIVE

OCEAN AVE.

Rustic Shelter

Caledonian Hospital (division of Brooklyn Hospital)

PARKSIDE AVE.

DRUMMER'S GROVE

WOODRUFF AVE.

The Pergola

Parkside Avenue
Ⓜ D

WEST DRIVE

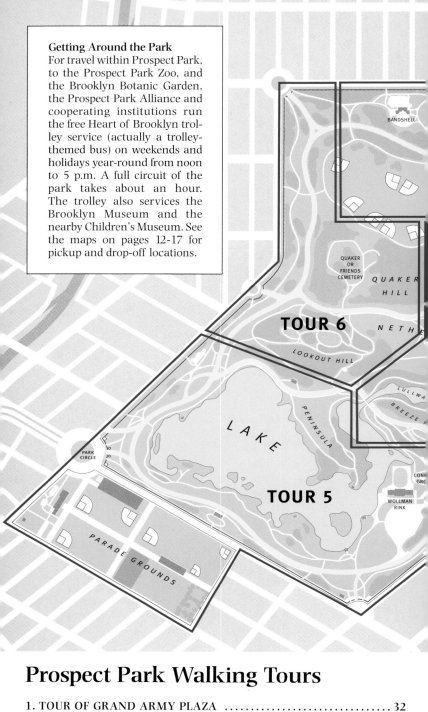

Getting Around the Park
For travel within Prospect Park, to the Prospect Park Zoo, and the Brooklyn Botanic Garden, the Prospect Park Alliance and cooperating institutions run the free Heart of Brooklyn trolley service (actually a trolley-themed bus) on weekends and holidays year-round from noon to 5 p.m. A full circuit of the park takes about an hour. The trolley also services the Brooklyn Museum and the nearby Children's Museum. See the maps on pages 12-17 for pickup and drop-off locations.

BANDSHELL

QUAKER OR FRIENDS CEMETERY

QUAKER HILL

TOUR 6

N E T H E

LOOKOUT HILL

LULLWA

BREEZE

L A K E

PENINSULA

PARK CIRCLE

TOUR 5

CON GR

WOLLMAN RINK

P A R A D E   G R O U N D S

Prospect Park Walking Tours

1. TOUR OF GRAND ARMY PLAZA 32
Soldier's and Sailor's Memorial Arch, Bailey Fountain, Statues of Kennedy, Skene, Warren, and Slocum, Park Entrance, Meadowport Arch

2. TOUR OF THE LONG MEADOW 40
Picnic House and Sullivan Hill, Tennis House, Upper and Lower Pool, Bandshell, Lafayette Monument, Litchfield Villa

3. TOUR OF THE RAVINE 50
Fallkill, Upper Pool, Ambergill and Ambergill Falls, Rustic Shelter, Boulder Bridge

4. TOUR OF LONG MEADOW EAST 57
Endale Arch, Vale of Cashmere, Rose Garden, Nellie's Lawn, Battle Pass, Nethermead, Binnenwater, Music Pagoda, Lullwater, Boathouse, Lullwater Bridge, The Camperdown Elm, Cleft Ridge Span, Terrace Bridge

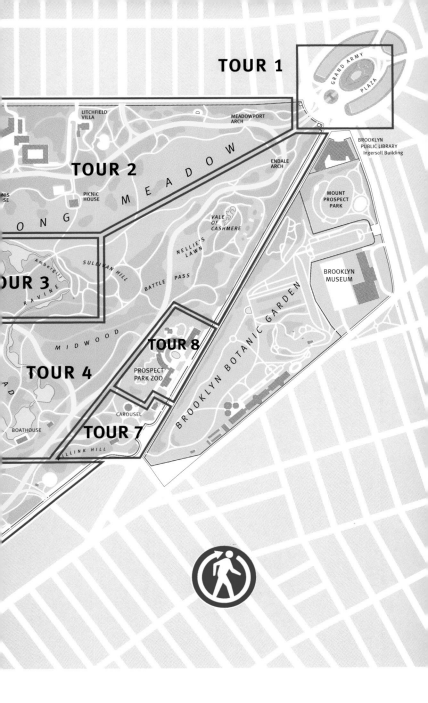

5. TOUR OF THE LAKE 71
Concert Grove, Oriental Pavilion, Sculpture in the Grove, Statue of Lincoln,
Wollman Rink, The Lake, Honor Roll Memorial, Drummers' Grove, The
Pergola and the Peristyle, Horse Tamers, Parade Grounds, Wellhouse,
Peninsula, Maryland Monument

6. TOUR OF LOOKOUT AND QUAKER HILLS 81
Lookout Hill, Quaker Hill

7. WILLINK TOUR 83
Willink Entrance, Carousel, East Wood Arch, Flatbush Turnpike Tollbooth,
Lefferts Homestead Children's Historic House Museum

8. TOUR OF THE PROSPECT PARK ZOO 87
The World of Animals and Discovery Trail, Animal Lifestyles, Animals in
Our Lives, Lioness Statue

ENJOYING THE PARK

Prospect Park is all at once a picnic ground, a nature walk, an ad-hoc athletic field, and a dozen other things depending on the visitor and the time of day and season. As such, the Parks Department has set out regulations for using the park that allow park-goers to enjoy its amenities without needlessly trampling the natural environment.

Picnicking and Barbecuing

Like its Manhattan counterpart, the lawns of Prospect Park are tremendously popular as picnic grounds, and have been since the park first opened. There are limited concessions facilities in the park (the snack bar at the skating rink will have a new counterpart in the Boathouse in 2002), but water fountains are plentiful and there are numerous hot dog vendors to be found along the periphery of the park.

Comfort stations are available near prime picnic grounds, including at the Picnic House and by the Parkside and Willink entrances. (See the maps on pages 12-17 for the locations of all rest-room facilities in the park.) Many of the facilities are also equipped for handicapped access.

Unlike Central Park, Prospect Park allows barbecuing on any of its open lawns except where prohibited by posted signs. In addition, designated barbecue areas have been set up adjacent to the Bandshell, alongside the Picnic House, and near the Wollman Rink, with a limited number of grills and large trash barrels for disposing of ashes. To avoid fire hazards, barbecue grills must never be set up within 10 feet of trees, and must be raised at least 3 feet above the ground. Coals should be doused with water and placed in tied trash bags with other garbage alongside trash barrels for parks workers to dispose of.

In addition, gatherings of 25 or more people need to obtain permits at least 30 days in advance from the Office of Special Events. Call 718-965-8969.

Rules for Dogs

Prospect Park is a playground for canines as well as humans, and specific rules have been crafted to make sure both species can share the space equitably. Dogs are allowed off-leash in the Long Meadow, the Nethermead, and the Peninsula Meadow at any time before 9 a.m., and after 9 p.m. in the warmer months (April through October) or 5 p.m. in the wintertime (November through March).

The Nethermead is also open to off-leash dog runs on summer weekdays after 5 p.m. Owners must keep their dogs supervised and in control and must pick up and dispose of all waste. Dogs are not allowed in playgrounds, on the bridle path, or on ball fields when games are in progress. Fines for noncompliance with these rules begin at $100.

Events

The Prospect Park Alliance hosts events in the park throughout the year, including the yearly "You gotta have Park!" festival (usually held in May) of family activities and volunteer park cleanup, and the fall "Green-A-Thon" walk and run to raise funds for park projects. For information about upcoming events, contact the park events hotline at 718-965-8960, visit the www.prospectpark.org website, or check the information boards located at most park entrances.

The Brooklyn Center for the Urban Environment, headquartered in the park's Tennis House, also runs frequent nature walks and other events in the park and surrounding communities. Contact BCUE at 718-788-8500 or online at their website www.bcue.org for a current schedule of events.

Fun for Kids

The **Prospect Park Zoo** is dedicated to exhibits geared toward teaching children about animals and their natural habitats. The zoo's centerpiece is its sea lion pool, where these playful sea mammals cavort in the water and sunbathe on land. Feedings are three times daily; call for the current times.

The **World of Animals** leads to the center's Discovery Trail, a selection of live animals shown in reproductions of their native habitats, along with interactive exhibits. Prairie dogs are accompanied by a "burrow" that children can climb into themselves, while a pond stocked with turtles and fish features metal "lily pads" that kids can walk on.

In **Animal Lifestyles**, children will find a variety of small animals, ranging from frogs, turtles, and birds to such exotic creatures as blind cave fish and Cape Rock hyrax, large guinea-pig-like rodents native to southern Africa. It also includes one of the zoo's largest and most popular exhibits: its Hamadryas baboons. In June 2000, a baby baboon was born to the pack, delighting park visitors.

Animals in Our Lives contains everyday animals including gerbils, chickens, pigeons, aquarium fish, and barnyard animals.

The Prospect Park Zoo is open 365 days a year, with children under 3 admitted free. (All children 16 and under must be accompanied by an adult.) For hours or other information, call 718-399-7339.

Just outside the south entrance to the Zoo is **The Carousel** featuring wooden horses as well as a lion, a giraffe, a deer, and two chariots adorned with fire-breathing dragons. Open for rides on weekends and holiday afternoons from April to October. Rides are 50 cents each, and there is wheelchair accessibility.

Sited midway between the Zoo and the Carousel sits the **Lefferts Homestead Children's Historic House Museum** dedicated to teaching kids about life in the 1820s and '30s, not just life for the Dutch family that owned the property, but for their Lenape Indian neighbors and their African slaves and later employees as well. Exhibits include a replica Lenape child's bed, lined with deerskin, and a re-created African child's bed, made of rope and straw.

The Homestead also offers a variety of games and storytelling for children, as well as a full season of post colonial-style gardening. The crop year begins with Linsey-Woolsy Weekend in the spring, when flax is planted; on the same day, the nearby zoo's sheep are sheared, and the wool brought to the Homestead for spinning. The flax is harvested in August, and made into linen in the fall, all at the Homestead. Harvest Fest, in September, and Winter Fest, after Thanksgiving, are other popular events, as is Pinkster Day, a re-creation of a Dutch and African-American celebration of spring that was widely celebrated in the colonial era.

Prospect Park features five **playgrounds** around its perimeter, at the 3rd Street entrance, 11th Street entrance, Vanderbilt Street entrance, and two beside the Lincoln Road entrance. (There is also a toddler's Tot Spot located just inside the Garfield Place entrance on Prospect Park West.) All five are recently renovated, with state-of-the-art safety surfaces and upgraded play areas and sprinklers.

The **Imagination Playground**, off Ocean Avenue and south of Lincoln Road, was redesigned in 1995 by park landscape architect Christian Zimmerman as a fanciful play area featuring a water-spouting dragon and other large sculptures for children to play on and around.

ACKNOWLEDGMENTS
The authors wish to thank

Administrator Tupper Thomas and the staff of the Prospect Park Alliance, in particular Historian/Archivist Julie Moffat, V.P. for Capital and Planning Mary Fox, and Director of Design and Construction Christian Zimmerman, ASLA, for their invaluable assistance.

President Judith Zuk and the staff of the Brooklyn Botanic Garden, in particular Director Emeritus Elizabeth Scholtz, Vice President of Science Steve Clemants, Director of Horticulture Jacqueline Fazio, Director of Publications Janet Marinelli, Public Affairs Coordinator Josie Phelps, Public Affairs Manager Wendy Brez, Horticultural Taxonomist Mark Tebbitt, Romi Ige and all the curators of the "gardens within a garden," especially Eric Andersen, Susan Aument, Scott Canning, Alessandro Chiari, Mark Fisher, Bill Giambalvo, David Horak, Robert Mahler, Rob Newgarden, Meghan Ray, Dan Ryneic, Nancy Seaton, and Ira Walker.

The staff of the Brooklyn collection at the Brooklyn Public Library

An array of articles, publications and books were also mined for information. But a special debt is owed to the following authors and their works:
Clay Lancaster, *Prospect Park Handbook* (Walton H. Rawls, 1967)
M.M. Graff, *Central Park/Prospect Park: A New Perspective* (Greensward Foundation, 1985)
Witold Rybczynski, *A Clearing in the Distance* (HarperCollins, 1999)
Francis R. Kowsky, *Country, Park & City* (Oxford University Press, 1998)
John J. Gallagher, *The Battle of Brooklyn: 1776* (Sarpedon Publishers, 1995)
Roy Rosenzweig and Elizabeth Blackmar, *The Park and the People* (Henry Holt, 1992)
Kenneth T. Jackson, ed., *The Encyclopedia of New York* (Yale University Press, 1995)
Edwin G. Burrows and Mike Wallace, *Gotham* (Oxford University Press, 1999)
Gregory F. Gilmartin, *Shaping the City* (Municipal Art Society, 1995)

Paul Keim of the Brooklyn Bird Club, John Muir of the Brooklyn Center for the Urban Environment, the organizers and performers of the Congo Square Drummers, and cartographer George Colbert.

The Creation of Prospect Park

Prospect Park is a little miracle: over 500 acres of meadows, lakes, and woods thriving in the middle of Brooklyn. Designed more than a century ago by the premier landscapers of the day, it still offers a rare combination of peaceful escape and urban energy. Over 6 million people visit its leafy environs every year, some just to take a break from the throbbing city, others to play soccer or baseball, join a birding group, take a ride on the carousel, or jam with the drummers who play there regularly. It is the borough's pride, "Brooklyn's jewel."

Prospect Park was conceived in the mid-19th century, when Brooklyn was embarking on its Golden Era. The Industrial Revolution was dawning in America; Brooklyn was a city in its own right, the third largest in the country, and growing. But though the idea for the park took shape in the late 1850s, construction did not begin until July 1, 1866.

In the intervening years, America had come through a great Civil War. And so the park was built by a city exultant to be again at peace, in a country no longer at war with itself. This celebration of union is one of the hallmarks of this great park.

Four structures within the park—the Boathouse, Peristyle, Lefferts Homestead and Litchfield Villa—have been placed on the National Register of Historic Places. In 1975, Prospect Park was designated a "scenic landmark" by the New York City Landmarks Preservation Commission, in recognition of the work of its creators in constructing a planned natural space the equal of any building in beauty, elegance, and grandeur. The entire park is now on the National Register of Historic Places.

"I see kids getting off of a yellow school bus or a trip on the subway with their teacher, and raising their eyes from their feet," says John Muir of the Brooklyn Center for the

1860 view from the Mt. Hope Reservoir looking west toward New York City across land that eventually became Prospect Park.

Urban Environment. "And some of them just can't resist to dance and skip and jump."

The Architects

The shape of Prospect Park as we know it today is largely the work of three forces: Calvert Vaux, Frederick Law Olmsted, and the Wisconsin ice sheet. We'll visit the junior partners first.

In 1866, the partnership of Olmsted and Vaux was close to finishing its greatest accomplishment to date: Manhattan's Central Park, which had revolutionized urban park design. In shaping a rocky wasteland into a world-class park filled with waterfalls and scenic vistas, the two partners had changed people's notions of what a park could and should be, and brought the phrase "landscape architecture" into the American mainstream.

Yet the Central Park project had been in many ways an unsatisfying one for Olmsted and Vaux. In particular, constant sparring with Board of Commissioners president Andrew Haswell Green over every expenditure had left the two tired and

James Stranahan: The man who dreamed Prospect Park into being.

frustrated with their work, and ultimately led them to resign as park architects in 1863. In 1865, Olmsted wrote to Vaux how much he wished the chance to design a park "with a moderate degree of freedom from the necessity of accommodating myself to infernal scoundrels."

Across the river in Brooklyn, James Stranahan was about to fulfill Olmsted's wish. A railroad contractor and builder, Stranahan had been looking at Manhattan's new park with undisguised envy. He had visions of making Brooklyn into a great metropolis. One day he hoped even to link it to New York via a bridge across the East River. But the fast-growing city had no significant parks to call its own. Residents had taken to strolling in Green-Wood

Calvert Vaux
Architect and Prime Mover

While Frederick Law Olmsted is known to many today, relatively few remember Calvert Vaux. But Olmsted's London-born partner was a brilliant landscape artist in his own right, nowhere more so than in Prospect Park. "But for his invitation," said Olmsted years later, "I should not have been a landscape architect. I should have been a farmer."

Apprenticed to a British architectural firm at the age of 19, Vaux traveled Europe to observe both historic buildings and rural settings. In 1850, he moved to Newburgh, New York to form a partnership with the greatest landscape designer of his day: Andrew Jackson Downing, one of the first to suggest a grand "central park" on Manhattan Island. Just two years later, Downing would lose his life when the steamboat *Henry Clay* caught fire and sank in the Hudson River, and Vaux moved to New York City to begin a practice on his own.

Downing, an advocate of designing houses to harmonize with their surroundings, found an able successor in Vaux, who went so far as to establish the natural as the central guiding force of rural architectural design. As Vaux wrote in his *Villages and Cottages:* "Woods, fields, mountains, and rivers will be more important than the houses that are built among them; and every attempt to force individual buildings into prominent notice is an evidence either of a vulgar desire for notoriety at any sacrifice, or of an ill-educated eye and taste."

While studying under Downing, Vaux was also exposed to works in the Victorian Gothic tradition then ascendant, which borrowed freely from Romanesque, Chinese, Egyptian, and Moorish motifs. The last of these would be particularly apparent in Vaux's work in Central and Prospect parks.

Neither park, though, might have come into being as it did if not for a fortuitous decision by Vaux to intervene in the project that his late mentor had helped bring about. In 1857, the clearing of land for Central Park had already begun, but

Cemetery for recreation. Stranahan wanted a park as a civic improvement, but also to draw the moneyed classes and so increase property values. He wrote of his hopes that a grand park for Brooklyn would "hold out strong inducements to the affluent to remain in our city, who are now too often induced to change their residences by the seductive influences of the New York [Central] park."

On April 18, 1859, the state legislature authorized funding for a new park, but without determining where exactly it would be built. Numerous sites were proposed, running from the town of New Lots east of the city to Bay Ridge to the south. But attention soon focused on a plot of land around Prospect Hill, a 200-foot-high pinnacle near the Brooklyn-Flatbush town line. The benefits of this site were many. A new park would provide fabulous vistas of New York City and its harbor; it would assure a clean watershed for the newly established Prospect Hill Reservoir; it could incorporate the nearby historic grounds where the Battle of Brooklyn had been waged, with its Sullivan Hill and Battle Pass; and as with Central Park, the mostly hilly land was largely undeveloped and undesirable for either housing or farmland. A new park, in short, could be constructed cheaply and with great scenic promise.

Moving the Park

To design Mount Prospect Park, as it was originally to be called, Stranahan at first turned to Egbert Viele, an engineer, who had been assigned to develop an initial design for Central Park before being shunted aside in favor of Olmsted and Vaux. Viele turned in a creditable design for a public grounds straddling Flatbush Avenue, with a broad carriageway leading up to a scenic overlook beside the reservoir. But in 1861 the Civil War broke out, and soon after, Viele was shipped out to the front. Work on a park for Brooklyn idled as the nation turned all eyes to the war.

By the time Stranahan's attention returned to the park site, he was

Calvert Vaux

Vaux judged the proposed design to be too unimaginative. He wrote to the park's board of commissioners suggesting that they open up the design to a public competition—a competition that then entered in partnership with Park Superintendent Frederick Law Olmsted. Meeting nights at Vaux's Manhattan home and often venturing out into the park site to survey the landscape by moonlight, the two drafted their masterful Greensward Plan, which combined many broad meadows with curved drives and paths harmonious with the natural landscape. While Olmsted focused on the day-to-day construction and plantings, Vaux tended to the park's structures: its bridges, arches, and rustic buildings.

After parting ways with Olmsted, Vaux turned his attentions more strictly to architecture, becoming one of the city's most sought-after architects. In collaboration with Jacob Wrey Mould, who had worked with Vaux on many of his designs for Central Park and Prospect Park, Vaux designed the first building of the American Museum of Natural History (Olmsted and Vaux had earlier designed the museum's grounds) and the Jefferson Market Courthouse, now a branch of the New York Public Library. He also worked on model homes for the poor. In the 1880s, he rejoined the Department of Parks for another stint as landscape architect.

In November 1895, Vaux took his usual walk to the ocean to view the setting sun. He never returned, having somehow drowned that evening in Gravesend Bay. He was 70 years old at the time of his death. In an obituary, William Stiles wrote, "In private life Mr. Vaux was a man of singular modesty, gentleness and sincerity, and while his learning and accomplishments gave him an assured position in the republic of letters and of art, his kindly and unselfish disposition endeared him to every one with whom he was closely associated."

determined to improve upon Viele's initial plans. He contacted Calvert Vaux and invited the architect to join him on a stroll through the proposed parkland. And so, on a cold January day in 1865, the two men slogged through the swampy ground to begin imagining a park.

After surveying the site, Vaux suggested an alteration in the park plan that would dramatically change the shape of the park to come. Flatbush Avenue, he noted had been built up as a causeway here to ease passage from the lowlands of Flatbush to the higher ground of Brooklyn. To have it running down the middle of the park would create "a barrier thirty feet high to all views between one piece of ground and the other." Instead, suggested Vaux, why not sell off the lands north of Flatbush Avenue and use the proceeds to buy up farmland in the flats south of the proposed park district, making one seamless property uninterrupted by intervening through streets? Stranahan agreed, and set off to convince the state legislature to allocate the necessary funds. (The northern section would later be developed as the brownstone neighborhood of Prospect

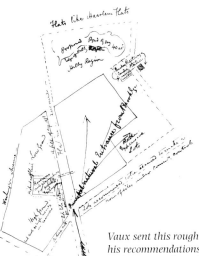

Vaux sent this rough map to Olmsted in California indicating his recommendations for the expansion of the park boundaries to the west and south of Viele's original plan. The map is oriented with south at the top.

Heights. Mount Prospect, which sat isolated on the wrong side of Flatbush Avenue, would become a small park of its own.)

As soon as it became clear that he would be hired to design the Brooklyn park, Vaux set about bringing in his old partner to help with the job. Olmsted was in California at the time, managing an unsuccessful gold mine at the foot of the Yosemite Valley. Vaux wrote to him repeatedly, urging him to return to the East. After months of cross-continental letters, Olmsted finally agreed, and the team was reunited for what would become their masterpiece.

Olmsted would contribute immeasurably to the design of Prospect Park, particularly in the specifics of the plantings and the Ravine's rocky waterfalls and narrow gorges that recalled his recent stay in California. While it's worth noting that the first detailed plans for Prospect Park were submitted in December 1865, just weeks after Olmsted's return from the West, the partners' ongoing correspondance had resulted in a true collaboration.

The Landscape

What Olmsted and Vaux found on arriving in Brooklyn was the work of a force of nature that has only appeared in temperate regions twice in the earth's more than 4-billion-year history. Eighty-five thousand years ago, the earth abruptly began to cool, in the last of a series of climatic oscillations known collectively as the Ice Ages. As the temperature dropped, the Wisconsin ice sheet started moving south from central Canada, gradually sweeping across Ontario and Quebec and finally covering all of New York State before it ground to a halt. It was global warming in reverse: The sea level dropped until the shore was miles out from where Coney Island would have been, if there had been a Coney Island.

Frederick Law Olmsted

Collaborator of Prospect Park

Frederick Law Olmsted's name is synonymous with parks. Born in 1822 to a prosperous dry-goods merchant and the daughter of a farmer in Hartford, Connecticut, Olmsted spent more of his youth wandering the woods and fields than in formal studies. "I was active, imaginative, impulsive, enterprising, trustful and heedless," he would later write. "This made me what is generally called a troublesome and mischievous boy."

Young Frederick did not attend college, either because of chronic problems with his eyesight (his contention) or his poor grades (as some historians believe). "While my mates were fitting for college," he wrote, "I was allowed to indulge my strong natural propensity for roaming afield and day-dreaming under a tree."

In his early adult years, Olmsted bounced from occupation to occupation: a clerk in a mercantile house, a year as an apprentice sailor on a shipping bark to China, and two abortive stints as a farmer, the first in Connecticut, the latter on Staten Island. (His Staten Island farmhouse from 1848 to 1854 still stands at 4515 Hylan Boulevard.) A budding journalist and ardent abolitionist, he traveled the South as a reporter for the *New York Daily Times*, reporting on conditions during the last years of slavery.

But Olmsted's love of parks was already coming to the fore. In 1850, he had toured Europe with his brother, talking with farmers and gardeners. He marveled at "the manner in which art had been employed to obtain from nature so much beauty." On his return, he authored a book entitled *Walks and Talks of an American Farmer in England*.

While in England, Olmsted also happened upon Liverpool's Birkenhead Park, laid out just six years earlier as one of the first true public parks. An essay on Birkenhead that appeared in *Walks and Talks* was included in Andrew Jackson Downing's journal *The Horticulturist*. Olmsted's descriptions of the rolling meadows and meandering footpaths of Birkenhead inspired Downing to add a postscript noting what a shame it was that New York had no such park.

Within six years, Olmsted had been hired as superintendent of construction for the park Downing had wished for Central Park. He came to the attention of

About 10,000 years ago, a mere eye blink in geologic terms—and a time when Native Americans were already colonizing the Eastern Seaboard in settlements now on the ocean floor—the glacier began to recede. Along the line of its southernmost advance, it had buried the onetime ocean floor beneath a mound of dirt, rock, and gravel 350 feet thick: a glacial moraine.

Prospect Park sits astride this Harbor Hill Moraine, as the Brooklyn section of the terminal moraine is called. The woodlands and meadows of its western fringe feed off the rich soil dropped behind the moraine by the retreating glacier. The hills, dubbed the Heights of Guan in colonial times, are the moraine itself. (Guan, or Gowan, was a Native American who lived by the nearby marsh that would also come to bear his name: Gowanus Creek.) The southeastern third of the park—the land added by Vaux—sits on outwash plain, the crushed rock and gravel that poured off the melting glacier to form the southern half of Long Island.

The varied terrain—over 560 acres of meadow, forested hills, and flatland—was perfect for Olmsted and Vaux's desire to create a range of naturalistic experiences. They wrote of wanting to fashion "first, a region of open meadow, with large trees singly and in groups; second, a hilly district, with groves and shrubbery; and third, a lake district, containing a fine sheet of water, with picturesque shores and islands. These being the landscape characteristics, the first gives room for extensive playgrounds, the second offers shaded rambles and broad views, and the third presents good opportunities for skating and rowing."

Upon surveying the site of their planned Long Meadow, Olmsted and Vaux noted with pleasure that "a large body of trees already exist

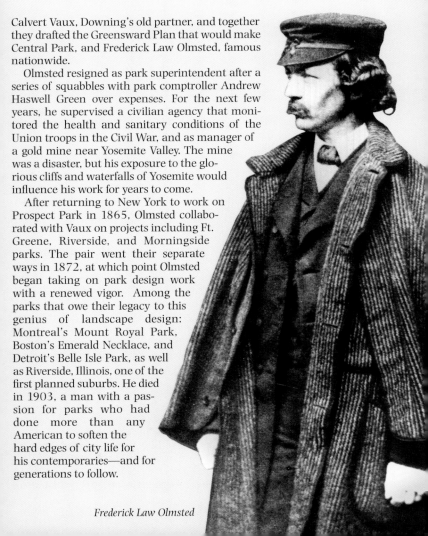

Calvert Vaux, Downing's old partner, and together they drafted the Greensward Plan that would make Central Park, and Frederick Law Olmsted, famous nationwide.

Olmsted resigned as park superintendent after a series of squabbles with park comptroller Andrew Haswell Green over expenses. For the next few years, he supervised a civilian agency that monitored the health and sanitary conditions of the Union troops in the Civil War, and as manager of a gold mine near Yosemite Valley. The mine was a disaster, but his exposure to the glorious cliffs and waterfalls of Yosemite would influence his work for years to come.

After returning to New York to work on Prospect Park in 1865, Olmsted collaborated with Vaux on projects including Ft. Greene, Riverside, and Morningside parks. The pair went their separate ways in 1872, at which point Olmsted began taking on park design work with a renewed vigor. Among the parks that owe their legacy to this genius of landscape design: Montreal's Mount Royal Park, Boston's Emerald Necklace, and Detroit's Belle Isle Park, as well as Riverside, Illinois, one of the first planned suburbs. He died in 1903, a man with a passion for parks who had done more than any American to soften the hard edges of city life for his contemporaries—and for generations to follow.

Frederick Law Olmsted

upon it, not too old to be improved, yet already old enough to be of considerable importance in a landscape." Oak, hickory, and chestnut trees covered much of the uplands, while red maple, sweet gum, and sour gum were scattered across the lowlands.

The meadow itself was more or less in place before Olmsted and Vaux started their work: As they wrote in their initial survey, "a space of two or three hundred feet in width..., of undulating ground, not wholly ungraceful, and now covered with a ragged turf." This they widened by removing brush and trees from its edge and shaped it into a breathtaking meadow nearly a mile in length. A small kettle pond became, with the addition of a waterfall fed by a newly sunk well, the beginnings of a mountain stream that wound its way through a designed ravine. And the desolate Flatbush farmland that Vaux had insisted be included in the park became a 60-acre lake, complete with winding shorelines and forested islands.

Still, Olmsted and Vaux were adamant that their work in Prospect Park was primarily to augment the existing landscape, not replace it. "No hill, not previously marred by excavations in street construction, has been leveled or its general elevation reduced," wrote Olmsted in 1871. "The tendency of all the changes of the surface has been to enlarge and make more distinct the

original natural features. Swamps, pond-holes, and hillocks which obstructed the general flow of the surface, alone have been obliterated."

The Construction

In addition to his role as co-designer, Olmsted was appointed supervisor of the park construction crews. Commuting daily by ferry from his home on Staten Island, Olmsted threw himself into the job, directing 1800 workers in moving earth, laying paths and drainage pipes, and planting more than 70,000 trees and shrubs. Many of these new plantings, particularly in the Long Meadow, were relocated from elsewhere in the park with the aid of a tree-moving machine that had been newly invented by assistant engineer John Culyer. By use of the device, parks workers were able to rearrange the park's scenery on an unprecedented scale: In 1872 alone, 284 trees were transplanted, including some of impressive size. By comparing growth rings on trees still standing with maps of the early park, arborists have estimated that some were probably 40 years old when they were moved.

To improve the sandy glacial till that made up the park's soil, Olmsted's crews added tons upon tons of peat dug up from the bogs dotting the future Long Meadow, plus such enrichments as horse manure, human waste, bamboo fiber, fish guano, lime, and marl. They also installed more than 50

John Culyer's invention was used to relocate hundreds of park trees, particularly around Long Meadow, to meet Olmsted's exacting standards of sightlines and view corridors.

Olmsted's construction crews moved mountains of soil to bring the new park into being. The future lake is at left, with Lookout Hill on the right.

rustic benches made of sassafras and cedar logs, along with 800 rustic birdhouses.

The Park's Opening

Prospect Park began drawing visitors even before it was finished. In 1868, more than 2 million people visited the park, though many of the trees were barely head-high and most of the "park" was still a construction site. By 1873, the numbers were above 6 million; by 1888, more than 10 million. Olmsted and Vaux's vision was an unqualified success. Not that success didn't come with its own problems. By 1885, Olmsted and Vaux were already complaining of erosion and trampled plantings from the incessant foot traffic, a problem that would persist into the present day.

The early reviews were likewise overwhelmingly positive. Charles Sprague

This rustic overlook, set atop the Ravine overlooking the Ambergill Pool, is to be rebuilt in coming years.

Sargent, the director of Harvard University's Arnold Arboretum, declared Prospect Park to be "one of the great artistic creations of modern times," calling it "an urban park unsurpassed in any part of the world in the breadth and repose of its rural beauty." The *Christian Weekly* observed, "Central Park, as any one may know who twenty years ago visited the waste wilderness which constitutes its site, owes its beauty almost entirely to art. Prospect Park, on the other hand, possesses rare natural advantages, which have been both skilfully and artistically developed."

If some of the park's boosters had designs on raising property values and promoting Brooklyn's growth, Olmsted and Vaux had in mind far loftier goals. By bringing all classes together in a beautiful naturalistic setting, they believed, a well-designed park could help promote a "democratic social order" in which rich and poor alike could escape from the stress and economic competition of everyday life. (Olmsted's own class biases played a role here as well, as he openly expressed his hope that the park would provide the lower classes with "the refinement and taste and the mental and moral capital of gentlemen.")

Changes to the Park

Both Olmsted and Vaux left Prospect Park in 1873, Vaux to go into architecture (starting with the design of the first American Museum of Natural History building in 1874) and Olmsted to take on the role of state parks commissioner. Each still kept close track of park developments, however, and were consulted occasionally on important issues. An early proposal to install a trotting racetrack along the western edge of the park was defeated by Vaux, who was backed by an outraged public that reportedly was set to riot if the plan had come to pass.

The most extensive additions to Olmsted and Vaux's original plan came at the tail end of the 19th century, when the renowned architectural firm of McKim, Mead & White was hired to redo the park's perimeter. While Olmsted and Vaux had preferred simple, unadorned entrances that highlighted the passage from the bedlam of the city to the peaceful calm of nature, McKim, Mead & White set about creating triumphal entrances in the Beaux Arts style of the day. The partners also

replaced the old wooden fence that surrounded the park with the stone wall or iron fences that remain today.

Other, less dramatic changes began in Olmsted and Vaux's time, and have been steadily and subtly transforming the park in the decades since. In 1885, the macadam paths began to be replaced with the hexagonal asphalt paving blocks that line some of the park paths today. When automobiles began displacing horse-drawn carriages, the gravel drives began to be covered with asphalt (first was East Drive in 1918). In 1926, all park drives were made one way to avoid accidents among speeding motorists, establishing the counterclockwise traffic pattern that endures today.

Gas lighting first came to the park drives in the 1880s, and by 1914, the entire park was fully illuminated at night by handsome cast-iron lampposts based on the 1907 design of Henry Bacon. None of the original fixtures survive.

The Moses Era

The next major era of change came to Prospect Park in the form of Robert Moses, who was appointed city parks commissioner in 1934 to go along with his existing title of head of the state's parks. (By the height of his power in the 1950s, Moses would also simultaneously control the Triborough Bridge and Tunnel Authority, the Housing Authority, and the City Planning

The 1890s brought classical designs to many of the park entrances, including Grand Army Plaza. Vaux's original fountain is visible through the arch.

Commission.) Moses first gained acclaim as a park builder, and did much to change the face of Prospect Park, adding many asphalt-covered play areas to the park, situated near entrances where they could easily be reached by neighborhood families. Moses's ideas for parks ran strictly toward recreation and away from the pastoral, however—the signature of a Moses park throughout the city remains a broad swath of asphalt—and so he ran roughshod over many of the designers' intentions, particularly in his construction of a new zoo on the former site of the Deer Paddock, and a skating rink that obliterated one of Olmsted and Vaux's most cherished vistas. Moses himself had written the bill appointing him city parks commissioner and had made sure it authorized him to remove buildings "incidental to park uses," a power he used to demolish Central Park's Casino and other historic structures. Park historian M. M. Graff alleged that Moses's disdain for Olmsted and Vaux's legacy was so great that when he discovered the designers' original drawings and documents in the cellar of Litchfield Villa upon taking office, he had them unceremoniously carted to the dump.

The Park Today

Over the past two decades, under the direction of Prospect Park administrator Tupper Thomas and the Prospect Park Alliance (a public/private partnership with the City of New York dedicated to improving the park), the park has begun to be restored to something like its original appearance.

Through a series of ambitious restoration projects, rustic shelters and bridges have been rebuilt, the entire ecosystem of the park has been restored, and visitors have increased from 1.7 million to over 6 million annually. Extensive programming and many educational and cultural programs provided by the Prospect Park Alliance, the Brooklyn Center for the Urban Environment, and Celebrate Brooklyn have brought Brooklynites back to the park.

And though wear and tear continue to take their toll, it is important to remember that even in Olmsted and Vaux's day, plantings were overturned and meadows turned to dust by the tramping of the millions of feet that came to visit each year.

A park, after all, unlike any other work of art, is to be used. And it's a testament to the skill and foresight of both the creators and their inheritors that Prospect Park continues to shine nearly a century and a half later, welcoming all New Yorkers to enjoy that "mood of unconfined contentment and delight" that is Prospect Park.

⊗ A Tour Around Grand Army Plaza

When Calvert Vaux and Frederick Law Olmsted first laid out their plan for Prospect Park, they envisioned a grand entrance that would provide a proper introduction to the park for visitors from the thickly settled regions to the north. That vision would become Grand Army Plaza, but not without a few bumps along the way.

The area then known simply as The Plaza was the first section of the park to be completed, in 1867. It had little to recommend it, though, aside from a simple fountain and a few sparse plantings. In their 1887 annual report, the park commissioners bemoaned, "The Plaza is certainly a total failure. No one cares to cross it. It is devoid of all life and is a stony waste. It is suggestive of Siberia in winter and Sahara in summer."

The Soldier's and Sailor's Memorial Arch

That would all change abruptly two years later. That year, John H. Duncan, already famous for his design of Grant's Tomb in upper Manhattan, was commissioned to carry out the plan of Brooklyn mayor Seth Low for a triumphal arch to honor the defenders of the Union during the Civil War. (An earlier idea to mark the site with a "huge drum surmounted by emblematic figures" was thankfully abandoned.) The cornerstone of the arch was laid by Civil War general William Tecumseh Sherman in 1889, and on October 21, 1892, President Grover Cleveland presided over its official unveiling.

Duncan's Memorial Arch stands 80 feet high and 80 feet wide, with an interior arch height of 50 feet. Its granite faces are thickly covered with carved images of fruits of sea and land, eagles, and ships' prows. The spandrels above the arch's south face bear reliefs of a pair of reclining winged figures—the whole ornate structure celebrating the power and prosperity of the victorious Union. Civil War veterans raised funds for its construction, with the state kicking in an additional $250,000.

The arch is also the base for a series of bronze statues celebrating the Union victory, but these were not installed until several years later. In 1896, the young sculptor Frederick MacMonnies (see sidebar, page 36), already famous for his fountain of

Columbia Enthroned, which had wowed audiences at Chicago's Columbian Exposition in 1893, designed the triumphal quadriga that tops the arch. The quadriga, an ancient Roman motif of a chariot pulled by four horses abreast, became in MacMonnies's interpretation a chariot bearing the great seal of the United States surmounted by a depiction of Columbia, who holds a sword in one hand and a flag in the other. Columbia, an allegorical figure representing the United States, is

carried majestically in her chariot of victory led by the herald of Peace. A pair of winged Victories blow trumpets to announce her arrival. Cast in forty pieces, the quadriga was assembled atop the arch by workers perched seven stories above the pavement. In October 1976, a severe windstorm almost blew the entire assemblage from its moorings, but it was rescued and secured at the last moment.

On the side of the arch facing the park are other prominent sculp-

John H. Duncan's Grand Army Plaza Memorial Arch, topped with Frederick MacMonnies's triumphal quadriga, has become one of Brooklyn's most enduring symbols.

tures, the Army and Navy groups, also designed by MacMonnies. The Army Group, on the arch's western (left-hand) pedestal, depicts a heroic scene of battle, with dead and dying soldiers, one of whom is being carried off by an immense winged Valkyrie, and, at the front, an officer

The Army Group (Western Pedestal)

This massive bronze statue, officially titled The Spirit of the Army, was intended by sculptor Frederick MacMonnies to honor the Union Army for its achievements during the Civil War. MacMonnies said his design was inspired by the work of French sculptor François Rude, whose work he felt presented "a perfect balance between the expression of content and design, neither being sacrificed to the other."

At the front of the pack, a young officer (bearing a striking facial resemblance to MacMonnies himself) leads the charge, his sword held high. To his left, a soldier with a revolver and a canteen flinches as he takes a bullet, while another is crushed beneath a collapsing cannon; only the fife player accompanying them seems unmoved by their plight. On the opposite corner, meanwhile, the company's drummer is less able to ignore the battle ranging in close quarters: he, too, has been shot, and is crumpling to the ground beside his drum. Above the company floats a winged Valkyrie, who is carrying off a fallen soldier along with his broken sword.

When the Army Group was installed, the contractors realized that there was a

problem with the dimensions: the head of the fallen soldier at left, beneath the gun carriage, protruded beyond the 13- by- 9-foot area of the pedestal, and so ran smack up against the marble facing of the arch itself. To solve this problem, Parks Commissioner George V. Brower instructed workmen to saw about an inch off the back of the soldier's head, and the statue fit firmly into place.

The Navy Group (Eastern Pedestal)

The Army Group's naval counterpart, The Spirit of the Navy, is sparsely populated and relatively sedate by comparison to the chaotic violence of its Army neighbor. Its sailors stand at the ready on the deck of a disabled ship, its mast snapped in two in the fighting. The ship's wheel and dying sailors are clustered about the confined space, overseen by a Bellona that provides a counterpart to the Army Group's Valkyrie. Crouched in front is a young black sailor with a revolver, notable as a rare depiction of an African American in Civil War statuary.

En route from MacMonnies's workshop in France to its final destination in Brooklyn, the Navy Group had a bit of its own mishap at sea: A derrick on the steamship carrying the sculpture broke, sending it plummeting in a fall that left it in a state where, in MacMonnies's words, "the men's knees were shoved up to their neckties." After $5000 of emergency repairs—and a special permit allowing the more than 8-foot-wide sculpture to be carted across the Brooklyn Bridge, the Navy Group was at last installed in 1901 on the Grand Army Plaza arch, completing its collection of statuary.

Frederick MacMonnies

Sculptor Extraordinaire

Unlike those who immigrated to the New World to find a better life, Frederick MacMonnies was the rare Brooklyn native who found fame and fortune in Europe. Born in 1863, as a young man MacMonnies was fortunate enough to be apprenticed to the famous sculptor Augustus Saint-Gaudens, who would later recall him as "a pale, delicate...lad."

After learning what he could from Saint-Gaudens, MacMonnies set out to study at the important École des Beaux-Arts in Paris, where the delicate lad soon came to international attention as a first-rate sculptor with a bold, original style. His bronzes of James Stranahan for Prospect Park and Nathan Hale for New York's City Hall Park won early acclaim, but he became a household word for the tremendous *Columbia Enthroned* fountain he constructed for Chicago's Columbian Exposition in 1893—not least thanks to those who remained scandalized by its depiction of a bare-breasted Columbia.

MacMonnies went on to design numerous pieces for Prospect Park that are renowned for their flair and energy, including the Grand Army Plaza quadriga, the *Horse Tamers* at Park Circle, and the statue of James Stranahan. But none would provoke such a reaction as his mammoth *Civic Virtue* fountain in City Hall Park.

Featuring a nude man holding aloft a sword above a pair of busty mermaids (representing "civic vice"), the statue immediately caught the wrath of both Victorians and feminists—the *New York Sun* called it an act of civic indecency—and it was eventually carted off to the Queens Municipal Building. In 1923, MacMonnies was asked to design a bronze replica of *Columbia Enthroned* for Central Park, but he had been too badly burned by the response to *Civic Virtue* to risk the public outcry again. It was a sad finale for one of Brooklyn's most notable artists.

leading the charge, his sword aloft. This hero's face, it has been noted, bears a striking resemblance to that of its creator, Frederick MacMonnies.

On the opposing pedestal stands the Navy Group, a marginally more sedate grouping of sailors astride a battered ship, its mast sheared off and rigging askew. MacMonnies himself is absent from this group, but many of the sailors were reportedly modeled after the sculptor's friends. To hoist the immense statue into place, a team of horses was hitched to tremendous pulleys, which lifted the huge bronze statue slowly into place atop its 13- by 9-foot ledge. When this operation was completed, on April 13, 1901, the arch and its statuary were at last complete.

Not all the arch's adornments were left to MacMonnies. On the interior of the pedestals are mounted bronze relief panels of Lincoln and Grant astride their horses. The riders were sculpted by William O'Donovan, while the horses were left in the care of Thomas Eakins, the famed portrait painter who sometimes turned his talents to sculpture. The panels were poorly received at the time—one 19th-century local wag reportedly gave the opinion that the reliefs were bad enough to belong in Central Park. They drew special disdain from modern-day park historian M. M. Graff, who wondered why Lincoln appeared to be "holding out his hat as if begging for pennies."

Inside the monument, iron stairs with stone treads decorated with military motifs—for example, the balustrades are Roman battle-axes—lead up to an open space over 25 feet high that was conceived as a room to house war trophies. Unused for many years, art exhibitions are now mounted here in the spring and fall by the Prospect Park Alliance. The arch is also open afternoons in the spring and fall to visitors who want to climb the stairs to the viewing platform at the top.

The overall effect of the arch is reminiscent of Paris's Arc de Triomphe in grandeur and in traffic confusion. The best way to approach the arch is to cross from the corner of Union Street and Prospect Park West, then hopscotch across the traffic islands until arriving safely on the plaza's central island. An alternate pedestrian route is to head south from where Vanderbilt Avenue intersects the oval, then make one's way past the fountain to the arch.

A Parade of Fountains

Just north of the arch, across a narrow band of asphalt and down a shallow flight of worn granite steps, is the Bailey Fountain. The fountain is actually the fourth to appear on this site. The original fountain, a simple jet of water, was roundly criticized in the local papers as inappropriate for such a grand space. In 1873, it was replaced by the Plaza Fountain, designed by Vaux, which featured a cast-iron dome equipped with 24 colored glass windows lit by gas jets, and horizontal and vertical jets of water. In front of the fountain stood H. K. Brown's statue of Lincoln holding the Emancipation Proclamation, which now stands in the park's Concert Grove.

Vaux's fountain was replaced in 1897 by an even more spectacular display: the Electric Fountain. Designed by Philadelphia electrical engineer F. W. Darlington, this massive construction was lit by 19 "automatic focusing lights," powered by the then modern marvel of electricity. The lights were controlled by an operator who directed his charges from a sunken bunker at the base of the fountain. The 75-year-old Olmsted, then a park consultant, gave his blessing to the fountain's placement, since it would be in the plaza, not the park.

The Electric Fountain ultimately fell victim to a more prosaic wonder of the modern age. In the early years of the 20th century, construction of the IRT subway through the plaza wiped out the central oval, fountain and all. Only a circle of bare turf remained to mark the spot for more than a decade.

In the late 1920s, the space was renamed Grand Army Plaza to commemorate the Union army's Civil War victory of six decades earlier. Shortly afterward, the current Bailey Fountain was installed in its central location. This fountain, sculpted by Eugene Savage on a design by Edgerton Swartwout, features a garish collection of allegorical and mythical figures, including conch-wielding mermen, a pot-bellied Neptune, and male and female nudes representing Wisdom and Felicity. The fountain is badly in need of repair: the ground around it has settled in recent years, and one of the mermen is in storage awaiting the fountain's restoration that will begin in the summer of 2001.

Statues of Kennedy and Skene

The tour of the central plaza's statuary is completed with the bust of John F. Kennedy to the north of the fountain, where the Lincoln statue once stood. The bust, by Neil Estern, is inscribed with the martyred President's famous phrase, "Ask not what your country can do for you. Ask what you can do for your country." Completed in 1965, it also bears a dedication by then borough president Abe Stark, a lifelong Brooklynite who is today better remembered for his political career than for his earlier occupation: as

The Electric Fountain, installed in 1897, featured 19 electric lights and a display of dancing waters that could be controlled by a conductor.

Union General Gouverneur Kemble Warren surveys the park from his perch at Grand Army Plaza.

Statue of General Warren

On the opposite wing near the arch stands a single bronze statue, almost overwhelmed by the 10-foot-high pedestal it rests on. This is a life-size sculpture of General Gouverneur Kemble Warren, a 19th-century army engineer, created by German-born sculptor Henry Baerer in 1896. (Gouverneur was the general's given name, not his elected title.) Warren's claim to Civil War fame was serving as chief topographical engineer of the Union Army at the Battle of Gettysburg, where he supervised the defense of the hill known as Little Round Top against the assault of Robert E. Lee's troops on July 2, 1863. His statue, as befits a surveyor, shows him armed only with a pair of binoculars. A carved note at the back of the pedestal states that it includes stone quarried from Little Round Top.

Statue of General Slocum

The final piece of statuary in the plaza sits at the head of the eastern berm, facing into the park at the arch's left-hand flank. It was sculpted by MacMonnies in 1905 to memorialize General Henry Warner Slocum, a Union general in the Civil War who led the successful defense of Culp's Hill at Gettysburg. Typical of MacMonnies's taste for high

a clothier whose "HIT SIGN, WIN SUIT" advertisement adorned the right-field wall of the Brooklyn Dodgers' Ebbets Field.

The earthen berms that form the "wings" of the plaza have over the years collected an assortment of monuments honoring less famous historical figures. Facing Kennedy from across the roadway is the bust of Alexander J. C. Skene, a 19th-century gynecologist and president of Long Island College Hospital who during his career invented 31 surgical instruments. On the outside of the eastern berm, affixed to a pink granite boulder, is a relief honoring Henry Maxwell, a longtime president of nearby Long Island College Hospital.

Stanford White's granite pavilions and cast-iron urns (since replaced by reconstructed replicas) provide a formal entrance to the natural wonders of the park.

drama, it depicts the general atop his horse, sword held high and hat askew. His horse appropriately displays the raised front leg, a symbol of victory.

Slocum, though a household name in the years following the Civil War, later became associated with tragedy when an excursion steamboat bearing his name caught fire in the East River on June 15, 1904, killing more than a thousand women and children from the Lower East Side's then thriving German community. A memorial to the victims now stands in Manhattan's Tompkins Square Park.

The Park Entrance

Even as John H. Duncan and Frederick MacMonnies were remaking the plaza, McKim, Mead & White were busily transforming the adjacent main entrance to Prospect Park. Most prominently, White placed four 35-foot Doric columns, topped with bronze eagles with wings spread, astride the entrance. (Matching stone eagles perch atop the columns' fascias.) Behind these and delineating the park's edge is a low granite wall with matching benches, which White topped with 14 bronze urns, their plantings guarded by entwined snakes that formed the urns' handles. Several of the originals were stolen over the years, and the rest were placed in storage. The cast-iron urns that now adorn the entrance are modern replicas.

Behind this low wall are a pair of 12-sided granite pavilions, also of White's design. These were built to shelter waiting streetcar passengers, as the plaza was a major 19th-century public transportation hub. The

Meadowport Arch, with its twin-arched design, makes for dramatic views of the Long Meadow. The arch design itself recalls Moghul Indian motifs.

original marble windbreaks, however, did not hold up very well under the elements, and were replaced by granite during the 1990s.

Leaving the City Behind

Enter the park from Grand Army Plaza on the path to the right of the drive. Passing beneath an American elm whose branches dip almost to touch the path, the visitor is presented with an immediate choice, as the path diverges around a European beech.

The path to the left ascends a small hill, atop which originally stood the Rustic Shelter, a sassafras-log structure that provided a shaded lookout to the Long Meadow beyond. Its only remaining memorial is a notch in the curbline marking its former site.

Descend the hill again, and the path meets back up with its twin to the right. Barely 100 paces into the park, you have already begun to leave the city behind. To the right, an earthen berm blocks out the surrounding streets, and the sounds of nature begin to dominate: the rustle of wind in the treetops, the gentle sound of songbirds.

Meadowport Arch

Round the bend, and you approach Meadowport Arch, through which you can just catch a glimpse of a sunlit meadow. Pass through, and the glimpse becomes a vista. There, laid out in front of you, is a rolling meadow stretching beyond the edge of sight, framed by trees of every variety and height. The Long Meadow—"the emerald sea," as one early parks commission report called it—seems to stretch on forever. Perhaps nowhere in the park does one get a better sense of what Olmsted termed the "enlarged sense of freedom" the weary city dweller gets when passing from the crowded urban environment into the calm, cool greenery of a park.

⊛ Tour of Long Meadow

The Long Meadow is well named. Nearly a mile in length and covering 75 acres, it is thought to be the longest stretch of unbroken meadow in any U.S. park.

If the ground on the Long Meadow is damp when you visit, that's because much of it sits atop the remnants of peat bog that once filled the park site. During construction of the park, Olmsted and Vaux had much of the peat dug out and used to improve the soil elsewhere in the park. More bogs may underlie much of the existing Long Meadow. A layer of peat—the remnants of a prehistoric pond—was discovered in the 1990s during construction for the Third Street playground.

Into this soggy soil, Olmsted and Vaux set the tremendous sandstone Meadowport Arch. From its Long Meadow side, the arch's ingenious design becomes still more apparent. By placing the tunnel at a 45-degree angle to the roadway above, Vaux was able to create a dual archway on its eastern end, not only providing a pleasant shelter from rainstorms

but creating a 180-degree panoramic view of the meadow beyond. The circular arches are topped by matching curved cornices, perhaps inspired by Moghul architectural motifs in India; inside, cedar planks carefully restored in the 1980s to the original specifications form both a warmly lit arched roof and a barrier against damp.

The north end of Long Meadow is the undisputed social center

Sheep grazed on Long Meadow in the park's early years, both for their pastoral quality and to save on lawnmowers. They were ultimately banished by city Parks Commissioner Robert Moses in the 1930s.

The Long Meadow in its early years, viewed from its north end. Despite the passage of 130 years, the sweeping vistas envisioned by Olmsted and Vaux remain almost unchanged today.

for the adjacent neighborhoods of Park Slope and Prospect Heights. On a typical summer afternoon, the rolling turf is carpeted with sunbathers, picnickers, kite fliers, kids playing soccer and Wiffle ball, and grown-ups playing softball and Frisbee and volleyball and occasionally such exotic activities as cricket. In the 19th century, Long Meadow was also the site of one of Brooklyn's grandest public spectacles: the Sunday School Anniversary Parade, held every year in the last week of May. In 1887, 100,000 people turned out to watch the children's parade and the maypole festivities.

In the early years of the park, sheep roamed this section of Long Meadow. As they had in Central Park, Olmsted and Vaux provided for sheep to graze on this meadow, both as a pastoral element and as natural lawn mowers. (A photo in the park's 1898 annual report was captioned, "Good Pasture Makes Fat Sheep.") The sheep and their attendant shepherd were finally banished by Robert Moses in the 1930s. These days, the only four-legged beasts to roam the meadow are dogs. This is a favorite gathering place for local canines and their owners, especially before 9 a.m., when hundreds of pooches can be found romping on the grass.

The rolling lawn that leads off to the west of Long Meadow was for decades the Croquet Grounds. To provide protection from the elements for the players, a Croquet Shelter was erected between the meadow and the West Drive. As of the park's centennial in 1966, a restoration of the ruined shelter was still planned, but it caught fire in 1979 and was demolished.

On the small forested knoll beside the onetime Croquet Grounds stands the Boy Scout Marker Monument, a simple bronze tablet mounted on a granite boulder. The original plaque, reading, "In Remembrance of Theodore Roosevelt, the Boy Scouts of the Prospect Heights District Planted These Trees," was installed in 1919 but disappeared at some point over the following decades, leaving only the bronze pins used to hold it in place. It was replaced with a replica in the 1980s.

As for the trees, they're almost all gone, felled by Dutch elm disease. The epidemic, which is believed to have originated in the Himalayas, was first identified by scientists in Holland in 1917, where it had arrived in shipments of wood from the

Dutch East Indies. Reaching the New World two decades later in crates made from infected wood, Dutch elm disease has since ravaged elm trees all over the North American continent. Once infected with the Dutch elm fungus by boring beetles, elms can spread the disease via their root systems, sickening an entire grove in a matter of years. Of the trees that were planted here in 1919, only one specimen remains. Park arborists are now engaged in an aggressive campaign to remove diseased roots and inoculate the tree with beneficial root fungi to try to save this last remaining elm.

Picnic House and Sullivan Hill

Follow the meadow south from Roosevelt Hill to a small clearing ringed with picnic tables. From the park's earliest days, this was a favorite site for New Yorkers hungry for greenery. As early as 1868, 75 picnic parties received permits for gatherings of 100 or more people in the still unfinished park's woods and meadows. By 1874, the number of permits had grown to 449, and by the 1880s the park had a national reputation as a preeminent picnic ground.

To accommodate this influx of visitors, the Picnic Shelter was erected in 1876 on a hill beside the central Long Meadow. Built of wood atop a brick foundation, the structure provided shelter from summer storms, as well as first-aid facilities, rest rooms, and a refreshment center.

Standing to the south of the Picnic Shelter in its early years was the park's carousel, an octagonal rustic structure that was relocated

from the Children's Playground in 1885 to be nearer the many picnicking families that flooded Long Meadow. With 24 wooden horses and 4 coaches, and towed by a team of real horses, the carousel was a popular attraction in the 19th century, especially among picnickers, who could buy tickets at half price. A second carousel replaced the original in 1915 but burned down 18 years later. The park would not get another until 1952, at its present location on the park's eastern edge.

The original Picnic Shelter was soon inadequate for the increasing flood of picnickers descending on the park, but lack of funding delayed action for almost half a century. In 1926, an oil stove at a hot-dog stand in the building blew up, and the entire structure burned to the ground. Two years later, it was replaced by the Picnic House, which still stands today. Unlike its rustic predecessor, this building is a massive two-story brick structure that onetime park curator Clay Lancaster described as looking like "a rural schoolhouse of the roaring twenties." The Picnic House now houses some of the park's permanent staff, in addition to providing rest rooms and a cold-drinks machine for picnickers. Its 3600-square-foot upstairs room is available for private parties and receptions.

In wintertime, picnicking on the meadow gives way to sledding. Children with a variety of homemade and store-bought toboggans have long descended Sullivan Hill, the steep slope with a broad, flat base that sits opposite the Picnic House. In the winter of 1915, a sledding course was briefly constructed from

The Picnic House replaced Olmsted and Vaux's original Picnic Shelter in 1928. It now houses Parks Department offices, in addition to supplying a comfort station and vending machines for picnickers.

Sullivan Hill to the Tennis House, with banked-snow sides and a runway that was watered to make for a faster track. The top of Sullivan Hill is currently fenced off as part of the Ravine restoration project, but sledding is still possible on the bottom part of the hill.

This site was originally called Sullivan's Hill, for John Sullivan, the American general who was captured near here by the British during the Revolutionary War's Battle of Brooklyn (see sidebar, page 62). But times change and memories fade, and in 1873 the hill was renamed for then noted actor John Howard Payne. A bust, based on an 1849 daguerreotype of the actor and capturing his "mild expression, with a 'shade more of sorrow than of anger,' " as one observer put it, was unveiled in a ceremony atop the hill on September 27, 1873, as a chorus of a thousand public-school children sang his signature tune, "Home, Sweet Home." Today, the hill is officially designated Sullivan Hill.

Trees on the Long Meadow

When construction on the park began in 1866, much of the area had been heavily logged for timber and to clear farmland, as well as for fortifications during the Battle of Brooklyn. At least one thicket of woods remained, however, an oak-chestnut forest along the park's western edge. It would become known as the West Woods. Many of these trees were left standing by Olmsted, while others were relocated to other parts of the park with John Culyer's new tree-moving device (see page 28). Studies of trunks of trees that have fallen, as well as core samples of standing trees, have found numerous specimens that predate the park, including a few that are as old as 300 years.

Picnicking in the park has been a popular pastime since it was first opened to the public. This clearing near the Picnic House is one of several where tables are laid out for visitors.

One of these old-timers is a white oak that stands at the southern foot of Sullivan Hill, near the newly restored bridge across the Ambergill. Unlike some of the top-heavy oaks in the more forested parts of the park, this tree has had little competition for sunlight, and so bears full branches that make it almost as wide as it is tall. In fact, its modest height belies its great age: In a 19th-century photo, it looks almost identical to its appearance today.

Further north along the slope of Sullivan Hill, note the numerous plantings of sweet gums, oaks, maples, and other native trees. Other recent plantings edge the path that runs in front of the ponds, and cut across the meadow near the Tennis House. These are re-creations of the original designs of Olmsted and Vaux, according to careful study of historic tree surveys and old photos. Once the trees are full-grown, the meadow at the foot of Sullivan Hill will be a distinct clearing of its own, screened off from Long Meadow by a stand of trees. And the sweeping view clear to the south end of the meadow will be reduced to a tantalizing glimpse of sunlit meadow between mature trees—a perfect Olmstedian vista.

While the trees Olmsted and Vaux planted in these sites have disappeared over the years, others have appeared in places they never intended. The grove of American elms on a knoll by the Upper Pool (formerly Swan Boat Lake) were likely planted in the 1930s, and is one of the few collections of the species in the park to have survived the onslaught of Dutch elm disease. These majestic trees are now some of the most imposing in the park— the down-sweeping branches of the elms by the pond are especially dramatic from a vantage at the south end of the meadow—and will be allowed to live out their natural lives. Once felled by disease or old age, however, they will not be replaced, and the meadow will be allowed to return to its original design.

Tennis House

South of the Picnic House, the Long Meadow broadens into a wide, flat expanse, much less hilly than at its northern end. It was here that the spread of one of the great sporting crazes of the late 19th century began: lawn tennis.

In the early 1880s, the sport of tennis exploded in popularity, with women in particular heading in droves to any open green space to set up an impromptu net. At the peak of the craze around the turn of the century, 300 lawn-tennis courts covered virtually the entire Long Meadow. A crew of parks workers laid out courts and cut and rolled the turf. Games were free of charge to

When lawn tennis became all the rage in the 1890s, parks workers laid out courts on the Long Meadow, available at no charge to men, women, and children.

The arched colonnades of the Tennis House, near Long Meadow, now shelter the home of the Brooklyn Center for the Urban Environment.

anyone who applied for a permit. All the equipment necessary for this much activity had created a storage crisis: The available space at the Picnic Shelter was jammed beyond capacity, as were lockers at Litchfield Villa, the Carousel, and the Music Pagoda.

Clearly, another building was needed. It arrived in 1910 in the form of the Tennis House, designed by Helmle, Huberty, and Hudswell,

whose principal, Frank Helmle, had spent a year working with the McKim, Mead & White architectural firm before starting his own practice. The Tennis House was placed on a knoll between the meadow and West Drive, near the Ninth Street entrance. (Olmsted's disdain for organized athletics in his parks was apparently put on hold for the occasion, but he wasn't happy about it. The designer is believed to have

selected the site himself, while working as a park consultant in the closing years of the 19th century.) In its basement were nearly a thousand lockers available to both organized tennis clubs and members of the general public for a rental fee of just 50 cents a year.

A colonnaded facade supports delicate arches, topped with a red tile roof, in a neoclassic style very similar to McKim, Mead & White's work in the park. The interior is made of limestone with Guastavino tile vaulting, one of four buildings in the park that utilize Guastavino tiles, a high concentration of this well-regarded structural technique. The classic architectural style clashed with the rustic look preferred by Olmsted and Vaux but is certainly a handsome edifice, peeking out from among the trees that border the meadow.

The Tennis House was beautiful, useful—and twenty years too late. By the 1920s, the lawn tennis craze had dissipated, and the lockers soon went mostly unused. The building, twice renovated in the 1970s and 1980s after a fire and vandalism, is now the home of the Brooklyn Center for the Urban Environment (BCUE), which since 1978 has conducted school programs and walking tours to educate the public about their natural environment. For a list of upcoming events, call 718-788-8549 or check the BCUE website at www.bcue.org.

The south end of Long Meadow would later be turned over to another sport, this time under more controversial circumstances. In 1959, with the Parade Grounds undergoing renovations, Parks Commissioner Robert Moses decided to make accommodation for the various adult and children's baseball leagues that used the park. He constructed five fields covering the meadow from its south end to the Tennis House. Unlike the temporary chalked courts of a half century earlier, these diamonds were permanent installations, with brick bleachers and a chain-link fence surrounding the entire complex. Local residents complained bitterly that Olmsted's vision was being ruined, but to no avail.

The chain-link fence and bleachers were finally removed in the 1980s and the ball fields resituated to minimize their visual effect on the sweep of the Long Meadow. The ball fields are now an integral part of Prospect Park, serving a variety of

The restored Upper and Lower pools are home to a rich ecosystem of lake plants, water-loving trees, and flowers. At right, one of the "swan boats" that plied the surface of the Upper Pool in times past.

youth and adult softball and baseball teams. To find out about enrolling a child in Little League, contact Prospect Park Baseball at 718-965-3741. For softball permits for all other leagues or individual teams, call 718-965-8943.

Upper and Lower Pool

Opposite the Tennis House, at the bottom of a long, low grade, is Upper Pool, (once known as Swan Boat Lake.) The descendent of a glacial kettle pond, it was landscaped by Olmsted and Vaux into an elegantly curving pool, adding a second pond to its north. Originally named the Pools, this lake was called Swan Boat Lake by park visitors in the first decade of the 20th century, when whimsical pedal boats, with wrought-iron seats and a carved swan at the stern, were rented there. At a dime an hour (half that for kids), the "swan boats" were an inexpensive alternative to the pedal boats on the Lake, then renting for 25 cents an hour. (If nothing else, they were a pleasant substitute for the pond's original attraction: the Circular Yacht, a "water carousel"

that went around and around under power of sail and oar.) The swan boats are long gone now, along with the Swan Boat House, a 20- by 30-foot colonnaded pavilion that once stood beside the pond. Through extensive restoration and replanting the lakes have begun to more closely resemble their original appearance.

The Western Perimeter

Continue south past the ball fields, then cross the West Drive on the path that curves west past an enormous European beech, its gnarled bark smoothing to satin as it reaches the upper canopy. This would be an ideal place for one of Vaux's arched underpasses, but instead the path and drive cross at grade, resulting in one of the park's 12 traffic signals. This is not by design, but rather the result of a historic happenstance.

When Vaux first recommended to

railroad contractor and Parks Commissioner James Stranahan that he expand Prospect Park to the south, there was one potential obstacle. While the farmland on the outwash plain could be bought up cheaply enough, the proposed park's western flank between what was then Ninth and Tenth avenues was owned by two of Brooklyn's most prominent citizens: Edwin Litchfield, a railroad magnate and land speculator who had bought up much of the farmland that was to become the upscale suburb of Park Slope; and Hugh McLaughlin, the powerful boss of Brooklyn's Democratic party machine. Litchfield and McLaughlin had bought these properties with dreams of turning the fertile farmland into mansions and villas for the city's growing upper crust, and they had no intention of giving up their land without a fight. (Vaux, it seems, knew what was to come: on an early sketch of the park site (see page 25), these western properties are marked simply, "Rather Expensive Lots.")

These properties, about 12 acres, were finally bought in 1869 for the then hefty sum of $1.7 million (about $20 million in today's dollars). But the lengthy delay had taken its toll. By the time Olmsted and Vaux were ready to tackle the western lands, the Panic of 1873 was on, and the parks commissioners were out of money. As a result, this area was left largely undeveloped as late as the 1880s, and its design was not as well integrated into the rest of the park—as evidenced by the fact that the paths and drives in this section cross each other at grade, even where underpasses might be expected. The delay also forced some hasty revisions in Olmsted and Vaux's design: Original plans for a zoo on this site were abandoned, and the West Drive was shifted slightly eastward into the park, creating a block-wide strip of parkland from Third Street to Prospect Park Southwest that was somewhat segregated from the rest of the park.

Follow the path as it forks south through a scattering of oaks and some rather impressive ginkgos, and past a small meadow, much of which was torn up in the 1930s for the construction of the IND subway line. (The ground here occasionally rumbles underfoot from the passing F trains to and from Coney Island.) The park's western edge terminates at Bartel-Pritchard Circle, a traffic circle that also marks the boundary between the neighborhoods of Park Slope to the west and Windsor Terrace to the south. The circle was renamed in June 1922 for Emil J. Bartel, Jr. and William J. Pritchard, Brooklynites killed in World War I. A marker was promised but not installed until more than 40 years later, when a local bus driver named Arthur Schneider launched a campaign for its erection. The dark stone monument in memory of the neighborhood's World War I dead now stands in the center of the circle, its inscription reading, "For Valor & Sacrifice, 1966."

The park entrance at Bartel-Pritchard Circle is flanked by a pair of giant granite pillars, topped by what appear to be huge bronze lanterns. Designed by Stanford White, these were modeled after the 4th-century B.C. Acanthus Column of Delphi. They were erected in 1906, but White never lived to see them. He was shot and killed earlier that year by Harry Thaw, the millionaire husband of his presumed mistress, Evelyn Nesbit. White died

Couples sway to the music of Boyd Raeburn and his Orchestra on a warm July night in 1953 at the Prospect Park Bandshell. This was one of the many name band dance programs co-sponsored by Con Edison and the Department of Parks.

The Lafayette Monument, dedicated May 10, 1917, is both a memorial to the American Revolution general and a commemoration of U.S.-French friendship.

in the roof garden of the old Madison Square Garden building that he himself had designed.

The Bandshell

Retracing your steps to the north, you soon come upon the park's bandshell. Standing in what was once an archery grounds and later a hockey field, it was installed in 1939 by Parks Commissioner Robert Moses, and was designed by Aymar Embury II, creator of the Central and Prospect Park zoos. The bandshell had fallen into disuse by the 1960s, but a pair of renovations in recent years have once again made it the focal point of music and theater in the park. The Celebrate Brooklyn festival, held every summer since 1979, brings local and international music, film, dance, and spoken-word performances to the bandshell from June through August; for further information, contact Celebrate Brooklyn at 718-855-7882, ext. 52, or visit their website at www.celebrate-brooklyn.org.

To the north of the bandshell and its neighboring playground is a small section of turf that has been designated a park barbecue zone, with some fixed grills and heavy metal trash cans for disposal of ashes. (Barbecuing is allowed in a number of areas but grills must be kept 3 feet off the ground and at least 10 feet away from overhanging branches of trees.) The barbecue zone has been a matter of some local controversy in recent years, with some residents of nearby Prospect Park West complaining of the smell. A more urgent problem is the damage caused by careless barbecuers who have set up too close to trees in this area.

The Lafayette Monument

The Ninth Street entrance is dominated by an enormous granite stele fronted by a bronze relief honoring the Marquis de Lafayette, the French statesman and soldier who gave vital support to the American forces during the Revolution. Sculpted by Augustus Lukeman and designed by Daniel Chester French (who also designed the allegorical figures of New York and Brooklyn now at the entrance to the Brooklyn Museum), it was dedicated May 10, 1917 by Marshal Joseph Joffre, French military commander on the western front during World War I, before "multitudes of school children" in a display of wartime patriotic fervor.

Lafayette, dressed in the garments of a general in the Continental Army, stands gripping a sword, its tip worn almost golden from the wear of many curious hands. Behind him, his African groom holds the reins of his horse a bit uncertainly.

The relief is set within an architectural frame set on a base and platform designed by architect Henry Bacon, who was collaborating with French at the time on the Lincoln Memorial in Washington, D.C.

Exit the park here and follow Prospect Park West to the north to circumvent the park's maintenance facility. This two-story brick stable and carpentry shop was built in the late 19th century to accommodate parks workers, and does the same today, though the horses have given way to trucks. At around the same time, a conservatory was built nearby to grow plants for the park and hold public showings. Its annual Easter lily display in the shape of a cross was once world-famous. These greenhouses were razed in 1955 by Brooklyn borough president John Cashmore, after Parks Commissioner Moses declined to pay the $650,000 it would have cost to repair them.

The Litchfield Villa

At the north end of this plot, just off Prospect Park West at Fifth Street, is the only mansion within the park boundaries: the Litchfield Villa. Litchfield had laid out his estate on the blocks bounded by Ninth and Tenth avenues and by Third and Fifth streets. To design the country home that he would place on the site, he hired the noted Hudson River estate designer Alexander Jackson Davis (a colleague of Vaux's old partner Andrew Jackson Downing) to build an Italianate villa that would harmonize with its natural surroundings. Finished in 1857, the villa was named Grace Hill, after Litchfield's wife.

After selling their land in 1869, the Litchfields continued to live in their home, which they leased back from the city, until 1882, when Mrs. Litchfield died and Edwin moved out. The parks commissioners moved in the following year, and the Litchfield Villa, as it is now known, has remained the park's administrative center ever since.

In its entrance lobby is a plaque designed for the park's Centennial in 1966 by Neil Estern, to honor the work of Olmsted and Vaux. A relief of the park's two designers, it welcomes visitors with the message: "This plaque commemorates the 100th Anniversary of Prospect Park. It is dedicated to the memory of its designers and builders Frederick Law Olmsted and Calvert Vaux. The park is their monument."

(29) A Tour of the Ravine

Both Olmsted and Vaux had spent time in the Adirondack Mountains shortly before beginning work on Prospect Park and had admired the rugged region's breathtaking plunges and sparkling cataracts.

The Italianate Litchfield Villa, built in the 1850s as the estate of Brooklyn landholder and railroad magnate Edwin Litchfield, now serves as the home of the Prospect Park administrator's office and the Prospect Park Alliance.

And so, with their characteristic aplomb, Olmsted and Vaux set out to re-create an Adirondack wilderness on a lumpy glacial moraine in rural Brooklyn. "Although we cannot have wild mountain gorges, for instance, on the park," wrote the designers in their initial report on the site, "we may have rugged ravines shaded with trees, and made picturesque with shrubs, the forms and arrangement of which remind us of mountain scenery."

To add moving water to their mountain tableau, Vaux and Olmsted took several of the kettle ponds on the park site (see sidebar, page 52) and expanded and connected them, forming a gravity-fed succession of pools and streams running from the Fallkill at the base of Quaker Hill to the 60-acre Lake at the park's southeastern extreme. Their stream would flow through some of the park's older woodland, a remnant of the oak-chestnut-hickory forest that once covered the entire

eastern United States. So dense were these woods that it was said a squirrel could travel from Maine to Arkansas without once leaving the treetops.

Olmsted planned for changing scenery along the path of the watercourse, beginning with "a series of pools, overhung on the one side by the trees upon the north-side of Friends [Quaker] Hill, and margined on the other banks by turf. It would then assume more of the usual character of a small mountain stream, taking a very irregular course, with numerous small rapids, shoots, and eddies, among rocks and ferns, until it emerged from the shadow of the wood upon a grassy slope then more quietly until, after falling over a body of rock...it would assume the appearance of a small river with high and shaded banks, and at length empty into the lake."

Olmsted's plans for a mountain ravine in rural Brooklyn didn't hold up too well. The sandy clay of the terminal moraine wasn't equipped

The Geology of Prospect Park

Prospect Park owes much of its natural beauty to the terrain on which it was built: towering heights (by New York standards, at least) and plunging hillsides. But go back in time 100,000 years, and there would have been nothing here but ocean floor.

The events that set in motion the creation of the park's landscape—indeed, all of Brooklyn and Long Island—began about 70,000 years ago when, for reasons not well understood, a glacier in central Canada began creeping south, growing slightly more each winter than it melted back in the summer. This Wisconsin ice sheet (named for the state where its effects were most pronounced) poured over all of eastern Canada and the northeast United States, pressing the existing terrain flat and scraping off much of its surface and carrying it along on its southward journey.

Central Park, which was entirely covered by the Wisconsin ice sheet, features many smoothed and grooved outcroppings of rock that were marked by the glacier's passage. Prospect Park has no such exposed bedrock, for one simple reason: In Brooklyn, the bedrock is buried far below the surface, beneath a pile of soil, rock, and gravel 350 feet thick. This is the Wisconsin glacier's "terminal moraine": The debris bulldozed up by tens of thousands of years of

southward movement and finally dumped here along the line of the ice sheet's furthest advance. So much ground-up glacial debris came to rest here, in fact, that new land masses were formed: Staten Island, Long Island (of which Brooklyn is a part geographically if not politically), Block Island, Nantucket, and Martha's Vineyard, and the long, curving arm of Cape Cod, none of which had existed before the ice came.

Resting as it does on the edge of the moraine, Prospect Park presents a dramatic contrast between that geologic structure and the outwash plain to the south, where a relatively thin layer of soil and gravel washed off the retreating glacier, forming today's Flatbush, Bensonhurst, and Coney Island. (Local geologists have noted that one can track the geologic history of Brooklyn through the subway system: Where trains travel belowground, they're within the thick moraine; where they're elevated or in open cuts, it's outwash.) The dramatic views from Lookout Hill, the plunging waterfalls and cascades of the Ravine—in each case, you're looking down off the moraine, standing as it were at the edge of the glacier as it ended its southward journey some 10,000 years ago.

When an enormous ice sheet begins to melt, it doesn't do so uni-

to withstand the steep slopes that the park's designers installed, and gradually collapsed, creating muddy bogs where they had envisioned quick-running rocky streams. The Ravine's woes were hastened by an ill-advised parks policy in the 1960s to strip wooded areas of their shrubs and ground cover to allay fears of crime. The resulting landscape was a moonscape of denuded soil, which soon became pitted with erosion gullies as rainwater stripped off the topsoil and carried it away, further clogging the waterways downstream.

By the 1980s, the Ravine watercourse was in a state of collapse. To bring it back, the Prospect Park Alliance launched in 1994 a 25-year-long, $43 million restoration

project for the area, fencing off a large area of parkland so that the woodlands could be replanted and have time to recover from a century of stamping feet and bicycle tires. Natural resource crews supervised by the Prospect Park Alliance planted 10,000 trees, 10,000 shrubs, 200,000 herbaceous plants, and 30,000 aquatic plants, all native. They have even gone so far as to dig out original boulders that had been buried in eroded mud, identifying them from historic photographs and carefully replacing them in their original orientation.

While restoring the Ravine, the current park designers are also hoping to improve it according to modern ecological principles. By creating a diverse natural forest in place of

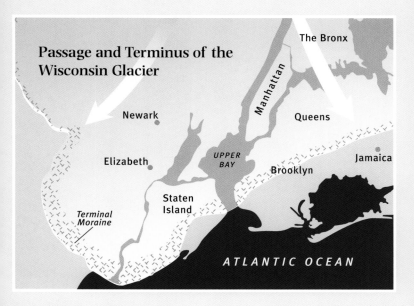

Passage and Terminus of the Wisconsin Glacier

The Bronx

Manhattan

Newark

Queens

UPPER BAY

Elizabeth

Jamaica

Brooklyn

Staten Island

Terminal Moraine

ATLANTIC OCEAN

formly. Chunks and great slabs of ice "calve" off the front of the glacier, and are often buried beneath more rock and dirt as the melting glacier relieves itself of its load. When these buried ice blocks melt, the ground above them collapses, leaving a kettle-shaped depression in the land above that is known to geologists as a kettle pond. The grounds of Prospect Park were littered with many small kettle ponds, and several survive to this day: Upper Pool, the Vale of Cashmere, and the Brooklyn Botanic Garden's Japanese Hill-and-Pond Garden all began life as kettles, the footprints of 10,000-year-old blocks of ice.

If Prospect Park lacks Central Park's exposed bedrock, it does share one characteristic with its Manhattan sibling: glacial erratics. These are boulders, often of considerable size, that were plucked from the earth along the glacier's journey and carried southward, finally being deposited here when the ice sheet melted. There are erratics scattered throughout the park, (the Music Pagoda is built atop a foundation of erratics collected on Sullivan Hill), and an even more impressive collection appears in the Brooklyn Botanic Garden's rock garden. There the stones have been labeled with plaques indicating their origin and the distances they were dragged by the ice before coming to land in Brooklyn.

Olmsted's mix of native and exotic flora, the hope is to produce an ecosystem that will eventually sustain itself—new plants and trees will grow up to replace those that die off, with minimal human interference. The Ravine restoration project has won several awards from the Art Commission of the City of New York, the New York City Landmarks Conservancy and ASLA.

Much of the natural ecosystem of the Ravine is now on its way to recovery—some of it in spectacular fashion. But most of the fences will remain up, as parks staff wait for the ecosystem to recover. They must also plan ways to allow the public access without destroying fragile plantings, a difficult task considering the limited city funds available

for maintenance. In the interim, parks volunteers and members of the Youth Council are conducting "Behind the Fences Tours" on weekends from April to November. Call 718-965-6988 to find out the current tour schedule.

Fallkill

To reach the beginning of the park's watercourse, enter the woodlands where the path from the Tennis House crosses the Long Meadow, beside a field of butterfly-strewn wildflowers just to the south of Upper Pool. (This path, fenced off entering 2001, is scheduled for reopening soon.) A few paces in, there is a puzzling sight: six parallel granite blocks set flush with the ground. These are the remnants of an original set of steps that were removed in the renovation in order to make the Ravine accessible to people with disabilities. The path was flattened and regraded, but the granite treads were left in place as a piece of the park's historic fabric.

A few steps more, and one reaches the Fallkill, the source of all the park's flowing water. (Kill, the Dutch term for waterway, appears in many New York-area place-names, and was a favored term of Olmsted's as well.)

Here a broad waterfall spills over a tumble of rounded boulders. These glacial "erratics" appear courtesy of the Wisconsin ice sheet, which dragged them tens or hundreds of miles before finally dumping them atop the moraine, where they were collected by Olmsted and Vaux for scenic purposes. (Most of Central Park's freestanding boulders are erratics as well; so is Plymouth Rock.) Many of the boulders had fallen into the Fallkill Pool just below by the time of the restoration; they have since been replaced to their original positions according to archival photos.

To the right of Fallkill Pool, at the base of the falls, grow a pair of European hornbeams, recognizable for their zebra-striped bark; these trees are also known as ironwood for their durability. Beside them stands a black tupelo, or sour gum, whose leaves in late autumn turn bright red, with dark blue fruits. At sunrise, the light playing over the rippling pool casts ever shifting patterns across the collection of foliage.

From the Fallkill Pool, the stream passes under Fallkill Bridge on its way to Upper Pool. This bridge is a re-creation of an original rustic wood structure designed by Olmsted and Vaux, which was replaced with a concrete structure in the 1950s. The restoration combines the best of both worlds: The logs adhere to the designers' rustic aesthetic, but look closely and you'll notice that the vertical logs are a two-piece wooden cladding; inside are steel posts. Likewise, the wooden walkway overlays a concrete base, to ensure that the bridge will withstand modern-day parks maintenance trucks.

Upper Pool

From here, the stream plunges over a small fall to enter Upper Pool, site of the most apparent of the changes resulting from the restoration project. Until recently, this linked pair of ponds was becoming rapidly over-

The beginning of the park's waterway: Fallkill Pool spills down from the Fallkill, past glacial erratic boulders and into the Upper Pool.

grown with a plant called phragmites (pronounced frag-MY-teez) that quickly came to crowd out many of the native species. As sediment washed down from the eroded hillsides and was trapped by the phragmites' roots, the ponds were slowly turning into swamps.

To restore this area, contractors drained the ponds, first relocating all the fish and turtles to the Lake. Then they dug down several feet, re-creating the deep pools of Olmsted and Vaux's day that had silted in over the intervening years. The path around the back of the lake has been edged with woodland plants, both to halt erosion and to create the soft-edged look that Olmsted and Vaux intended.

Native water lilies, arrow arum, and pickerel weed have replaced the phragmites, and blue flag irises bloom along the shore in the spring. A small peninsula has been converted into a nesting island for birds and turtles. Here, where the forest opens up to meet the pools, there is an interplay of dappled light and the sounds of running water and birdsong. Sweet gums and sour gums grow along the banks, including at least one sweet gum along the east shore of the pond that has been identified as original to the park. In autumn, these woods are a profusion of color, with bright scarlet sour gums and red maples mixing with the surrounding yellows and greens in a rich palette of natural tones.

In the pond restoration, park landscape architects placed three concrete "beaches" on the shoreline, on the site of original access points.

These were first established by Olmsted and Vaux to allow visitors to access the ponds without trampling the plant life, and reestablished today for the same reason.

In the few years since the restoration began, wildlife has been attracted in droves to Upper Pool's plentiful water and lush foliage. Migratory birds are everywhere in spring and fall, joining the pond's permanent residents: a flock of mallard ducks that no longer fly south each winter, preferring to remain on the frozen lake. In the summer, frogs by the dozens sun themselves on the lakeshore, as do turtles. One recent immigrant is Godzilla, a 38-pound snapping turtle bequeathed to the park by the Brooklyn Botanic Garden when it was renovating the pond at its Japanese Garden.

Ambergill

At Lower Pool's outlet, water exits via a splashing, noisy brook. It flows beneath Esdale Bridge, another restored bridge of rustic elements with a steel-and-concrete core, and into a stream dubbed the Ambergill by Olmsted in another of his whimsical moments. (Gill, a Scottish term derived from Icelandic, refers to a narrow, stream-filled glen.) This feeds a forested grotto known as the Ambergill Pool, which had completely silted in by the 1970s to form a swamp, and had to be dug out by a park contractor. Its shores now feature thick plantings, and turtles and green herons populate its banks.

If the gates are open (or you're with

a tour), you can follow the Ambergill along its left bank, with the steep slope of Sullivan Hill at your left shoulder. This landscape, once a rocky mud pile, is now a profusion of greenery: wild roses, raspberries, and blackberries. (The latter two, so closely related as to be almost genetically identical, are often classified together as brambles.) All of this has been replanted in recent years, restoring some of Olmsted and Vaux's vision of a Ravine that was "gay with flowers, and intricate and mazy with vines and creepers, ferns, rushes, and broad-leaved plants."

Ambergill Falls

As the path winds its way around a thicket of low growth, the sound of rushing water becomes apparent. Round a bend and you're upon it: Ambergill Falls, a torrent of water plunging between sheer rock walls, then wending its way downstream among thick foliage.

To look on it now, you'd never know that until recently, there was nothing here but a muddy flat strewn with a few rocks, the stream a mere trickle. Archival photographs existed of a waterfall in the park in the 19th century, but no one was certain where it had been. Then the director of landscape management, Edward Toth, noticed that a set of

Ambergill Falls as it appeared in Olmsted and Vaux's original creation. This scene was painstakingly re-created from original photos in the 1990s, with workers shoring up the stone retaining walls with concrete to prevent future erosion.

standing boulders in the foreground of one photo corresponded with the boulders that rim Rock Arch Bridge. Years later, when the construction crews began digging, they soon uncovered the original stonework, which had fallen in and become buried as the soil gave way over decades of wear and erosion. The newly restored falls are now buttressed by hidden retaining walls.

Rustic Shelter

Up the steep stone steps that face the waterfall—themselves recently restored, with many of the original stone steps recut and jigsawed together to repair damaged sections—is a rustic shelter, a re-creation of one of those that originally dotted the park. This open-topped, octagonal structure has been built by craftsman Dennis Madge out of cedar and tamarack logs, using pegs and dowels but not a single nail. The shelter is topped by a wooden birdhouse. Another original shelter is scheduled to be reconstructed along the path that leads west from this spot, perched above the Ravine.

Boulder Bridge

Behind the rustic shelter is Boulder Bridge, a tall, narrow span that straddles the bridle path. (It can also be reached via the path that climbs the north flank of Sullivan Hill.) Built in the late 19th century to replace a wooden bridge on the site, it is entirely local in origin, built from glacial erratic boulders collected on the site.

Just north of Boulder Bridge once stood the Dairy Cottage, an early focal point of park picnickers. Nineteenth-century life was full of fears of such urban ills as cholera and tuberculosis, and fresh milk was considered a perfect symbol of rural purity. The sheep and cows that pastured on Long Meadow were housed in a stable here, and milk was dispensed to any and all parkgoers—11,000 quarts in the summer of 1871 alone. Fresh foods were also available for order, including cold beef, ham, and tongue sandwiches, and pickled oysters.

The Dairy resembled Vaux's design for a similar building in Central Park—twin gabled wings and a steeply pitched roof with a cupola. It also held storage space for picnic supplies and a pair of "retiring rooms," or rest rooms. To provide further facilities for a day in the park swings and picnic tables

This newly rebuilt rustic shelter near Boulder Bridge features an open octagonal design with wooden benches and a birdhouse overhead.

were placed nearby.

But with the construction of the Picnic Shelter on the opposite side of Long Meadow in 1876, the Dairy's days as the park's primary resting point were numbered. Instead this area became the park's first permanent Menagerie, beginning with bear pits in 1890, and gradually accumulating buildings throughout the early years of the 20th century. All these buildings, including the Dairy, were razed in 1935 when the new zoo opened on the opposite side of East Drive. The one exception was the Elephant House, which survived into the 1980s as a storage facility.

Back on the path by the falls, head downhill toward the Nethermead Arches at the Ravine's foot. You now enter the thickest part of Prospect Park's forest, and in parts the oldest as well. The woodland giants here are white, red, scarlet, and black oaks, hickory, black birch, black beech, tulip trees, and sweet and sour gums. On the left of the path as it descends, just below the stairs to the rustic shelter, stands a tulip tree that is believed to be older than the park itself. Listen for the sound of woodpeckers rattling trunks, and keep an eye out for the chipmunks and frogs that habituate the newly lush underbrush.

Before restoration began, this stretch of waterway had become the resting place for much of the sediment that had washed downslope from the surrounding hills—so much so that ground level had reached the base of the thin oak on the left bank of the stream, about 40 feet above Nethermead Arch. As the contractors dug out the streambed, they discovered one of Olmsted and Vaux's original weirs, which now splash unobstructed once more. The gurgling sound, it was discovered, had been enhanced by building a hollow into the rock to amplify the sound of the water and send it booming over the arches below. Other weirs were reconstructed based on archival photographs.

Much of the replanting occurred as recently as 1999. In some places, one may still see the erosion control matting that is being used throughout the park to keep damaged soil in place. As foliage sprouts up through the matting, the coconut-husk mesh gradually decays, leaving only the ground cover that has grown up through it.

A Tour of Long Meadow East

When Olmsted and Vaux sketched out their plan for Prospect Park, they knew they wanted the park design itself to draw visitors inward, away from the bustle of the city. They were also aware that since most parkgoers would begin from one entry point, Grand Army Plaza—then the only

corner of the park near heavily settled districts or public transportation—they needed to encourage park visitors to disperse as quickly as possible, to avoid a bottleneck of humanity at the entrance. So they designed a pair of main entry routes: Meadowport Arch, leading to the west side of the Long Meadow and the Picnic Woods; and Endale Arch, drawing curious feet into the park's eastern realms.

Endale Arch

Enter the park at Grand Army Plaza to the left of the drive, on the path running alongside MacMonnies's statue of James Stranahan. The path winds between beeches and pines before arriving at the mouth of another of Vaux's arches. Passing through the dark and cool of the stone arch, you arrive at the very north end of the Long Meadow. As author Tony Hiss writes in *The Experience of Place:* "The light seems almost to be converging on the meadow from all directions—tumbling onto the grass nearby and also glowing through the trees beyond the meadow." Whereas back at the park entrance, writes Hiss, the visitor might have sensed that the path continued on for a few hundred feet more, "Now, standing up at the north end of the Long Meadow, a stroller may feel that a much vaster scene perhaps repeats itself many

Endale Arch as it appeared to Olmsted and Vaux. Though most of its wood interior has disappeared over the years, it still provides a dramatic entrance to the Long Meadow.

The Vale of Cashmere, nestled at the bottom of a natural glacial hollow, offers simple fountains and brickwork paths as counterpoint to the natural beauty of its lush greenery.

times over, distance upon distance."

The park's current landscape architect, Christian Zimmerman, says that when he leads tours of the park through Endale Arch, "nobody says a word. They just stare. All you see is the park—there are no tall buildings, and all you see is this beautiful, pastoral landscape. And it just gets silent.

"Then," he says, "you hear the cameras start going off."

This arch was originally named Enterdale by Olmsted (since it provided entry into the dales and meadows beyond), but had already been shortened to Endale by the time of the park's completion. Here you can see how Meadowport Arch to the west appeared before its recent renovation: Most of the interior woodwork is gone, as is the original bench seating, leaving an arched stone ceiling whose echoes are popular with both children and neighborhood musicians looking for a euphonious practice space.

Endale Arch presented one of the park's more problematic construction challenges. When C. C. Martin, Olmsted's engineer in charge of building the arch, began preparing the site, his crew found what he later described as "a tenacious clay saturated with water," which extended several feet belowground. To make a firm foundation, Martin excavated from 8 to 16 feet of boggy soil, then buried a lattice of timbers and poured concrete to underlie the

arch, an experience that Martin would later put to use in sinking the pillars for the Brooklyn Bridge.

Take the path to the left that skirts the eastern edge of the Long Meadow. Before long, a set of steps will branch off to the left, almost hidden beneath a pair of lindens of rather unusual stature. At the top of these steps, beside the East Drive, once stood another of Olmsted and Vaux's shelters. Called simply enough the Shelter by Road Steps, it had disappeared by the 1930s.

Crossing the drive and turning right on the path, you find yourself skirting the edge of a forested precipice. This sudden plunge is a dramatic example of a glacial kettle, one of several in the park. When the Wisconsin glacier was done with its work of scraping off the face of New England and making Long Island out of it, the mammoth ice sheet began to melt. But it did not do so monolithically. Tremendous ice blocks were calved off the retreating glacier and subsequently buried under the flood of silt and muck that poured out of the melting ice sheet, forming mud-covered ice hummocks. When the underlying ice melted, the soil on top collapsed into a rounded depression in the shape of a kettle, which gave these geological features their name.

Vale of Cashmere

Turn and descend the steps into this steep valley, and you find the Vale of Cashmere, one of the rare formal spaces within the largely naturalistic park. In fact, the Vale was not part of the original park design and remains today the park's least authentic area. In the original plan, this was the site of the Children's Playground, an open lawn overlooking a small pond. On the hill to the east of the vale was a croquet lawn, a maze, and a 7-sided summer house. Toy sailboats could be launched on the pond. This was also the site of the park's first carousel, erected in 1874 but moved 11 years later to the Picnic Woods to take advantage of the greater crowds there.

The hillsides here were largely kept clear of trees by Olmsted and Vaux to provide an open vista in every direction except toward Flatbush Avenue to the east. The effect was apparently not quite what its designers had in mind: The 1893 report of the parks commissioners described it as an "arid waste...where the children never go to play." Despite its deficiencies, however, it had by then already acquired a new name: the Vale of Cashmere, after the setting of Thomas Moore's epic poem "Lalla Rookh," which reads, *Who has not heard of the Vale of Cashmere/ With its roses the brightest the earth ever gave.* Olmsted, for one, hated the affectation of the name, but it stuck.

Around this time, the Vale was transformed by the installation of pedestals and urns around the pond, the reinforcement of the shoreline with stone coping, and replacement of the original tar path with a brick walkway. This being the 1890s, a Frederick MacMonnies sculpture was all but required, and the Vale had perhaps the oddest one yet. This was a fountain depicting a nude boy, perhaps two years old, holding a squirming duck in his arms. Around him stood a circle of six spouting turtles. The fountain was dutifully

taken out of storage every year and installed in the Vale during the summer months, until it was stolen on October 14, 1941. A replica exists in the Metropolitan Museum of Art in Manhattan, though without the accompanying spouting turtles.

The Vale now features only a pair of simple fountains surrounded by lush growth, including many flowering dogwoods and azaleas. Just above the flight of steps to the south of the Vale stands one original element: a large native magnolia that predates not only the redesign but the park itself. The quiet, secluded pond is also a favored resting place for migratory birds, with warblers, orioles, and hummingbirds among those attracted to the peaceful site.

Rose Garden

Ascend the steps at the north end of the Vale, through a wooded area and into an open, formal lawn. This is the Rose Garden, which took the place of the Children's Playground in 1895 over Olmsted's protests. ("I beg leave to ask you to pause before making such a questionable departure from the established design of the Park..." the 73-year-old consultant wrote to parks commissioners that year.) Unfortunately, while the lily ponds in its center thrived in the damp heat, the roses didn't fare as well, and are long since gone. Dogwoods and yews now ring the pools.

The next change to the Rose Garden came in 1969, when Mayor John Lindsay had fountains installed in the central pools. These were inaugurated for a breakfast meeting of Lindsay's that September—then promptly turned off when the underground pipes began to leak, flooding the entire area. Though Parks

One of the Rose Garden lily ponds during the garden's heyday. The ponds have been dry since the 1960s.

The Nethermead Arches in an early woodcut. The Vaux-designed triple span cleverly separates footpath, Ambergill, and bridle path from the auto traffic on Center Drive, while providing a dramatic entry from the wooded Ravine into the open Nethermead.

Commissioner August Heckscher promised the fountains would be back in working order by the following spring, they have remained dry ever since.

Nellie's Lawn

Follow the path that exits the Rose Garden at its southern end until you see a large clearing off to your right. This is Nellie's Lawn, believed to be named for a local girl who would spend hours reading beneath an immense spreading elm that once stood here in the park's early years. When Nellie died (local legend doesn't say how), her friends memorialized her by hanging a sign with her name on the tree trunk; the Parks Department later took up her memory by planting beds of flowers in the lawn spelling out Nellie.

To the north of the lawn, a narrow corridor of lawn wends between the trees to the Vale of Cashmere beyond. Just to the left of this neck is an exceptional tulip tree, notable for its full, low-hanging branches. (Most mature tulip trees soar high into the air before their first branches appear, but this one does not, perhaps because outside of a deep-woods environment there is less competition for sunlight.) This provides an excellent vantage for the orange-and-yellow trumpet-shaped flowers that bedeck this tree every spring.

Across Nellie's Lawn to the west, the East Drive begins its plunge from the heights of the moraine to the outwash plain below. This was originally the line of the Flatbush Road—and before that, an

This bronze eagle marks the site of the Dongan Oak, felled by American Revolutionary soldiers to slow the British advance during the Battle of Brooklyn.

Indian trail—that marked the only easy route between the towns of Flatbush and Brooklyn. As such, it played a crucial role in that long-forgotten military confrontation that helped inspire the park's existence: the Battle of Brooklyn (see sidebar, page 62).

Battle Pass and the Site of the Dongan Oak

Though the battle was waged over a large swath of Brooklyn and neighboring towns, Battle Pass, as this notch in the hill became known, was the center of the fighting, and it is denoted by three simple markers. The first, secured to a boulder at the base of a large maple about 15 feet from the roadside, is the Line of Defense Marker, noting both the site of the rebel defensive lines and that of Valley Grove House, the tavern that stood on what is now Nellie's Lawn in colonial times.

Cross the drive to the recreation lane on its opposite side, and continue about 100 feet down the hill. There you'll find the Historic Marker of Battle Pass, which gives a somewhat sanitized version of the events of that long-ago day: "Here the American forces stood their ground against the Hessians coming from the

south till flanked from the river by a body of British troops. General Sullivan was captured, but most of his troops retreated across what is now the Long Meadow joining the Maryland and other troops for the final resistance near the old stone house of Gowanus."

Move another hundred feet downhill, then cross the drive again to where a bronze eagle stands atop a granite plinth. This monument marks the site of the Dongan Oak, a large white oak that stood on the border between Flatbush and Brooklyn in colonial times, and which was felled to block the British advance in preparation for the Battle of Brooklyn (see sidebar, page 62). On the battle's hundredth anniversary in 1876, a Centennial Oak was planted at the site. Though described as "thriving vigorously" 17 years later, it is now nowhere to be found.

To get a sense of the hill the British would have had to climb had they not found a way around the American defenses, ascend the steep flight of steps across the road from the Dongan Oak marker, heading into the Midwood. Keep climbing as the path creeps uphill through the dense forest, until finally you spot what appears to be a sunlit hilltop ahead.

Plunge on forward, and you find yourself not on a rise at all, but at ground level of the Long Meadow. You have just ascended the moraine. Imagine doing the same with no steps, no path, and a thick tangle of underbrush, and you can see why

the American troops believed they could hold off the British forces—until their plans went so dreadfully wrong.

The Nethermead

The Nethermead Arches at the foot of the Ravine provide more than just a scenic vista from the path that leads out of the park's shadowy woods. They are functional, separating the auto traffic (which would have been carriages, of course, in the park's early days) on Center Drive from the bridle and pedestrian paths that pass beneath it. The triple arches also provide a boundary and a link between two dramatically different landscapes, the wooded mountain defile of the Ravine and the open, grassy expanse of the park's centerpiece: the Nethermead.

The Nethermead is well named. Situated at almost the exact center of Prospect Park, it is utterly remote from the crowded urban streetscapes that surround the park. Its rolling meadows are not nearly so dramatic nor so crowded as the Long Meadow's. Even a summer Sunday will likely find a handful of Frisbee players and dog-walkers enjoying the broad lawn. The Nethermead is one of the few sites in the park where off-the-leash dog walking is allowed on summer evenings.

The Nethermead has some of the oldest trees in the park. At one time there was talk of x-raying them to search for embedded Revolutionary War bullets, although in recent years several have succumbed to the ele-

The Battle of Brooklyn

The Battle of Brooklyn—or the Battle of Long Island, as it is sometimes known—is not much remembered these days, unlike such momentous American battles as Yorktown or Gettysburg. But as the first major battle of the American Revolution, and the largest as well, it inaugurated a new mode of combat. "The battle," as historian John Gallagher would write, "marked the first step, however tenuous, into the modern era of 'total' war."

Howe's Plan of Attack

In August of 1776, the stage was set for open confrontation between the forces of the British crown and the colonial rebels. The Declaration of Independence had just been signed a month earlier, and tensions were high.

British commanding general Sir William Howe, who had been forced to evacuate Boston when the already entrenched American Army began growing in strength, turned to New York as a more inviting military base. New York lay astride key north-south supply routes and had a more divided populace than Boston's (Staten Islanders, in fact, would welcome the Tories with open arms). Howe hoped an attack on the city would make for "a decisive Action, than which nothing is more to be desired or sought for by us as the most effectual Means to terminate this expensive War."

A Fatal Error

Howe landed his 29,000 troops near Gravesend Bay on August 22, 1776. Defending the heights of Brooklyn were about 7000 men, under the command of General George Washington. Washington, however, was far back of the front lines, at a fortification at the intersection of today's Court Street and Atlantic Avenue in Cobble Hill. Direct command of the troops had been left to General Nathanael Greene, but Greene fell ill with typhoid just a week before the battle, and was replaced by generals John Sullivan and Israel Putnam, neither of whom were as familiar with the terrain on which the battle was to be fought.

Sullivan and Putnam focused their efforts on defending Valley Grove Pass, today known as Battle Pass and located in Prospect Park, placing 1300 soldiers at the narrow pass and cutting down trees to act as a blockade. The Dongan Oak, a great white oak that Governor Thomas Dongan had designated as marking the border between the towns of Flatbush and Brooklyn, was felled across the road as a final barrier to any British assault.

The Americans had similarly guarded Bedford Pass to the east, but in what was to be a fatal error, not Jamaica Pass far out in Queens County. British lieutenant general Sir Henry Clinton, alerted to this lapse by informants, quietly moved 14,000 troops along Kings Highway under dead of night in a column 2 miles long, leaving their campfires burning to throw off the Americans. They swept through the pass unopposed, then quickly overwhelmed a handful of sentinel horsemen along the Bedford Road (near the course of today's Atlantic Avenue). Arriving behind the American lines on the morning of August 27, Clinton's forces fired a pair of cannon blasts to alert the British and Hessian troops below Battle Pass, and they converged on the American forces in a deadly pincer maneuver.

The American soldiers, many afraid to surrender, reportedly because they'd been told they'd be killed, fought fiercely but were swiftly cut down; one Hessian officer noted that "The greater part of the riflemen were pierced with the bayonet to trees." Most of the survivors fled along the Port Road, a path that led across the present-day Long Meadow and to First Street, the Hessians firing carbines and cannon at their retreating backs. Sullivan himself was captured in a cornfield near Battle Pass, not far from the hill that bears his name.

Brave Fellows Lost

Meanwhile, the Maryland regiment led by Lord William Alexander Stirling, for whom Park Slope's Sterling Place is named, was trapped between an advancing British line near today's Fourth Avenue and the carnage behind them. Stirling's 400 men instead turned and charged the 2000 British troops dug in at the Old Stone House at Fifth Avenue and Third Street. Six times they charged, twice briefly gaining control of the house, but were cut to ribbons in the process: 256 of the Americans died, and all but 10 of the remainder were captured. Washington, watching the slaughter from afar, reportedly cried

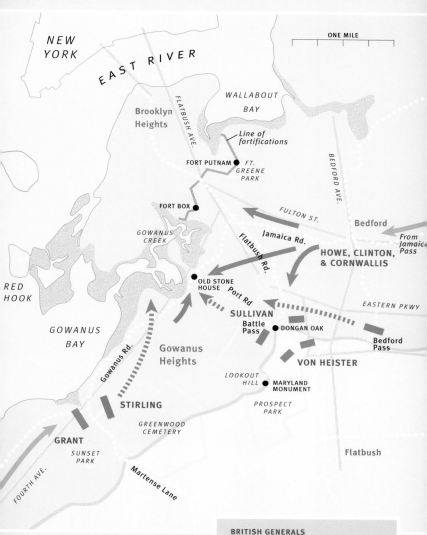

Map labels:

NEW YORK

EAST RIVER

WALLABOUT BAY

Brooklyn Heights

FLATBUSH AVE.

Line of fortifications

FORT PUTNAM — FT. GREENE PARK

BEDFORD AVE.

FORT BOX

FULTON ST.

Bedford

GOWANUS CREEK

Jamaica Rd.

From Jamaica Pass

Flatbush Rd.

HOWE, CLINTON, & CORNWALLIS

RED HOOK

OLD STONE HOUSE

Port Rd

EASTERN PKWY

SULLIVAN

Battle Pass

DONGAN OAK

GOWANUS BAY

Gowanus Heights

Gowanus Rd.

LOOKOUT HILL

MARYLAND MONUMENT

VON HEISTER

Bedford Pass

STIRLING

GREENWOOD CEMETERY

PROSPECT PARK

GRANT

SUNSET PARK

Flatbush

FOURTH AVE.

Martense Lane

---

out, "Good God! What brave fellows I must this day lose!" (The Old Stone House was demolished in the 19th century in a display of Gatling guns, but has been rebuilt today from the original stones, and serves as a historic center.) Stirling's charge did buy extra time for the rest of Washington's troops, however, who were able to flee to the defended battlements in Brooklyn Heights, and eventually to Manhattan.

At least 1000 Americans died in the Battle of Brooklyn. Many of the thousands who were captured would go on to die in the notorious British prison ships docked in the East River, their bones later reinterred beneath a memorial in Olmsted and Vaux's Fort Greene Park. The British, meanwhile, lost about 60 men in the battle. Brooklyn's farmers, driven out by the fighting returned that fall to find many of their homes and farms demolished in the fighting and their pastures littered with dead soldiers. As late as the park's construction almost a century later, according to one early report of the parks commissioners, "Balls and bones are frequently turned up by the workmen, in the progress of their excavations, marking the spot where the tide of battle surged."

The cascade of Binnen Falls, just north of the Boathouse, marks the transition from the mountain stream of Ambergill and Binnenwater to the more placid Lullwater and Lake.

ments. (Prospect Park arborists estimate they lose about 45 to 50 trees a year to weather, old age, or disease.) One of the most dramatic was a 300-year-old, 4-foot-thick elm tree that came crashing down in a vicious storm on November 9, 1972; the same storm uprooted a nearby tree, flattening a car parked on Center Drive, fortunately resulting in no serious injuries. Other signs of age are apparent in the remaining trees: A silver linden along the west path bears large trunk scars from branches that have fallen in recent years, as the tree's spreading limbs literally pull themselves apart by their own weight. To prevent a similar fate, the osage orange (named for the hundreds of bright green fruits that it sheds each autumn, as well as its orange-tinged bark) at the fork in the path has been fitted with steel bars to keep its forked trunks from splitting apart.

Binnenwater

The rushing stream from the Ambergill slows after passing beneath the Nethermead Arches to become the meandering Binnenwater. (Binnen, Dutch for "within," is yet another Olmstedian reference to the area's remoteness.) Today a narrow stream weaving between muddy banks, the Binnenwater was originally very different. Bending left after passing under the bridge, the stream entered Binnen Water Pool, a large pond 10 feet deep and 450 feet in circumference, making it nearly as large as Lower Pool. With a jetting fountain at its center, the pool provided a cool respite between Nethermead and the woods to the north, much as the Pools offer a shimmering attraction between Long Meadow and the Ravine. Further along, the Binnenwater flowed into the Lily Pond, a large pool that emptied into Binnen Falls.

The Binnenwater proved highly susceptible to siltation from upstream and had mostly filled in by the 1930s. Of the original weirs providing small waterfalls along the stream, several are now buried or in poor shape. (To see the extent of the silting, observe the large stones placed in the ground at the north end of Music Pagoda Bridge: These are the original shore of the Binnenwater, now a good 10 feet inland.) And some years ago, an underground pipe that led to the Lily Pond broke, creating a willow-filled swamp, half overgrown with shrubs and fallen trees, now all but forgotten behind the Music Pagoda.

The Binnenwater is scheduled for restoration beginning in the spring of 2002. The Binnenwater Pool will be cleared and excavated, the original weirs will be restored, and Music Pagoda Bridge will be rebuilt in rustic form.

Music Pagoda

Along with the gradual filling of the Binnenwater, another major change came to the Nethermead in 1887, when the Music Pagoda was constructed in a wooded area at the meadow's north end. Built atop a stone foundation, its narrow posts and a flaring roof are supposedly reminiscent of a Chinese city gate. Stones for the foundation, according to an early parks report, were collected on the "hallowed grounds of

Sullivan Heights" (a.k.a. Sullivan Hill); the base originally housed lockers for lawn tennis and croquet, both popular pastimes on the late-19th-century Nethermead.

To make way for the pagoda and its attendant Music Grove, a thicket of woods was cleared and replaced by a set of radiating paths—now visible only as sight lines between the London plane trees that grew up between them. The Music Pagoda quickly became the musical center of the park, playing host to Edwin Franko Goldman's long-running brass band. Goldman's concerts were said to be so popular in the 1950's that Brooklynites would shut off the Dodger game on their portable radios to listen. By the 1960s, theatrical productions had joined the Pagoda's menu, with one season offering performances of George Bernard Shaw's *Arms and the Man* and Lorraine Hansberry's *A Raisin in the Sun.*

In 1968, tragedy struck when the Music Pagoda caught fire, burning down to its stone foundation. It was rebuilt 3 years later, just in time to serve as the site of a large concert to protest the war in Vietnam. The Music Pagoda is now used about twice a week, most often by church groups.

Lullwater

To the east of the Music Pagoda, the path crosses over Binnen Bridge, another rustic bridge recently restored in concrete and wood cladding. The bridge spans Binnen Falls, which plunge down a clattering cascade into the Lullwater, where the narrow stream opens up into a broad waterway that continues all the way down to the Lake.

The Lullwater, as befitting its name, was designed to provide a placid stretch of calm. It meanders in a fashion reminiscent of the Serpentine in London's Hyde Park. After the rush of the Ambergill and Binnen Falls, it's a place to relax and watch ducks, swans, and turtles bask.

Olmsted, certainly, was pleased with the results. Some years after the park's opening, he wrote that the view from Cleft Ridge Span across the head of the Lullwater was "one of the most superb and refined park

Since the 1880s, the Music Pagoda has provided the setting for thousands of performances in its shaded setting just off the Nethermead.

scenes I ever saw—I believe it to be unequaled for a certain kind of sylvan beauty."

Beyond the bridge, along a small path that seems better suited for elves than full-size humans, is a low, shallow-roofed structure that is all but lost among its surroundings. This well-camouflaged building is a comfort station, built in 1888, one of the oldest masonry structures in the park.

The Boathouse

Further along, the Lullwater is dominated by the classical white facade of the Boathouse, another building dating from the post-Olmsted-and-Vaux era. The park's original boathouse was very different from today's in both form and placement. A canopied structure, it straddled the north end of the Lullwater on piers, spanning Binnen Falls and providing a view south across the Lullwater to the Cleft Ridge Span.

In 1905, this rustic building was replaced by a massive Beaux Arts structure designed by Frank J. Helmle and Ulrich Huberty, who would go on to design the Tennis House in 1910 on the Long Meadow. The new Boathouse was relocated to the Lullwater's eastern edge to provide sunset views across the water. Modeled after the lower story of

BOAT HOUSE—PROSPECT PARK.

The view from the Boathouse balcony (top photo) is a sweeping panorama taking in the elegant Lullwater Bridge (left) and the outflow from Binnen Falls. There, on the right, stood the original wooden Boathouse (postcard above), spanning the Lullwater and offering a close-up view of the falls. The current Boathouse (left) opened in 1905, and the white terra-cotta structure, modeled after the Library of St. Mark in Venice, soon became a favorite of local postcard-makers, not to mention the families that thronged its landing pavilion to launch rowboats and canoes. The boat concession has since relocated adjacent to Wollman Rink, and the Boathouse is presently being restored for use as the nation's first urban Audubon Center, with exhibits and interactive information kiosks. It will open to the public in the spring of 2002.

Sansovino's 16th-century Library of St. Mark in Venice, the stately building with its white terra-cotta facade and elegant balustrade quickly became a popular attraction with park visitors and was featured in many color postcards of the time. The Boathouse was granted landmark status by the city in 1968.

As with many of the park's structures, time was not kind to the Boathouse, and the city had briefly scheduled it for demolition in the 1960s. It was dissuaded by a storm of public protest, led by poet Marianne Moore and the then nascent Friends of Prospect Park. Instead the structure was almost entirely dismantled in 1971 and rebuilt with new terra-cotta facing. Unfortunately, the new facade proved not to be waterproof, and the building was closed again in 1997 for extensive repairs. To be reopened in the spring of 2002, some of the terra-cotta facing will have been replaced and the interior totally renovated.

The building's original function—as a boating center—has long since been usurped by the Lake. Over the years, the Boathouse has served as a snack bar and ranger station, among other functions. Now the reopened Boathouse will be the Prospect Park Audubon Center, the national Audubon Society's first urban center. It will also house a snack bar and gift shop.

Lullwater Bridge

At the same time as the Boathouse was built, Olmsted and Vaux's rustic stone-and-oak Lullwood Bridge was replaced by the Lullwater Bridge, a delicate iron structure that spans the water just downstream from the Boathouse. Standing by its metal balustrade, you can absorb at once the sights and sounds of the far-

The weeping branches of the Camperdown Elm, now surrounded by a protective fence, have been a favorite curiosity since the park's opening.

The iron Lullwater Bridge spans the duckweed-filled Lullwater just downstream from the Boathouse. Taking the place of the earlier stone-and-wood Lullwood Bridge, the current bridge provides pleasant views of one of the park's most charming waterways.

flung reaches of the park: a family of swans paddling downstream among the duckweed, the brilliant white Beaux Arts Boathouse behind you, the sounds of Binnen Falls and dogs barking.

The Camperdown Elm

Behind the Boathouse, on a gentle grade leading up to Wellhouse Drive, is one of Prospect Park's oddest and most interesting landmarks: the Camperdown Elm. This rare "weeping" elm defies all the usual laws of tree growth, its branches drooping down to almost brush the ground.

Its story begins in Dundee, Scotland, in the early decades of the 19th century. There, on the grounds of Camperdown House, a grounds-keeper discovered a Scotch elm tree that, instead of growing tall and straight, was "creeping along the ground amongst other elms." The tree, it turned out, was a mutation that lacked the gene for negative geotropism—quite literally, it didn't know which way was up, and so it crawled along the ground instead of soaring into the sky. (Similar genetic mutations can cause "weeping" in other trees, of which the weeping beech just north of the Boathouse is a good and nearby example.)

Many cuttings were made of the original Camperdown Elm, including one that was donated to Prospect Park in 1872. Since the Camperdown mutation never develops a trunk of its own, the tree was grafted onto a normal Scotch elm base; in a fortuitous side effect, this would also grant it immunity to Dutch elm disease. The tree was rooted in a mound of earth so that its downsweeping branches would clear the ground.

Like the Boathouse, the Camperdown Elm was in bad shape by the 1970s, having suffered from decades of neglect and decay. And like its Beaux Arts neighbor, the elm was saved largely by Marianne Moore, who wrote a poem in 1967 dubbing it "our crowning curio" and asked that donations be made to save it instead of sending flowers to her funeral. Major surgery was performed under the auspices of the Friends of Prospect Park, leaving the tree with notable scars—one large one is visible on the branch that grows south, toward the path leading to the Cleft Ridge Span. In 1998, the Prospect Park Alliance gave the elm a further rehab, recabling its branches and replacing its concrete fillings with an extruded foam that is lighter and less prone to collecting moisture, further reducing the stress on the tree's bowed branches.

The Cleft Ridge Span, cutting a path through Breeze Hill from the Lullwater to the Concert Grove, was opened in 1872, the last of Olmsted and Vaux's arches to be opened in the park. The Beton Coignet molded concrete interior, chosen for affordability as the hard economic times of the 1870s began squeezing the park budget, is a remarkable artistic achievement in its own right, adding to the exotic flavor of the arch's design.

Cleft Ridge Span

Behind Camperdown Elm sits the entrance to the Cleft Ridge Span, the last of Olmsted and Vaux's arches to be built in the park, from 1871 to 1872. With the park running short on funds, Vaux happened upon an innovation that would save money and be aesthetically pleasing: The arch is built not of stone, but of a cast concrete process called Beton Coignet that could be cheaply produced in patterned slabs.

This material, originally invented and patented in France, could be poured into wooden molds and embossed with highly detailed designs. It could also be colored in different shades. The Cleft Ridge Span is the first use of the Beton Coignet process in the United States.

Base of Breeze Hill

Turning right on the path before Cleft Ridge Span, one passes through an overgrown area between the wooded slopes of Breeze Hill and the Lullwater. This secluded zone is a favored habitat for birds and other animals, with chipmunks racing in and out of the lush undergrowth,

and swallows swooping low over the water to feed at dusk. It will soon be the site of nature trails beginning at the new Audubon Center, with informational signs about the historic and ecological significance of the Lullwater. Also scheduled is the reconstruction of a 100-foot-long rustic arbor along the path, where visitors will be able to rest on wooden benches and view the surroundings.

Terrace Bridge

As the path bears left to follow the curve of the Lullwater, you come upon Terrace Bridge, spanning this narrow valley. (While the valley looks original, it was actually constructed by Olmsted and Vaux's engineers and builders to their specifications).

Designed by Vaux to replace a temporary wooden structure, the bridge was the designer's final addition to the park, completed in 1890. Terrace Bridge is now a bit in decay—the original cast-iron tracery that filled the long triangles above the arches has long since been filled in with solid steel—but still majestic with steel arches beneath brick vaults. Through its massive archway, one can glimpse the final major piece of Olmsted and Vaux's Prospect Park landscape design: the Lake.

🎵 A Tour of the Lake

When the city of Brooklyn, at the urging of Calvert Vaux, purchased the farmland southeast of the original park site, it did more than just add to the park's size. It also provided the setting for perhaps the park's most sublime landscape: the Lake, 60 acres in size, a man-made wonderland that was to provide the park with a venue for everything from rowing to fishing to ice-skating. And it also provided the backdrop for the park's most elegant formal setting: the Concert Grove.

Concert Grove

When Olmsted and Vaux designed Prospect Park, they deliberately went for the naturalistic feel that they had achieved in Central Park: a melding of meadow, forest, and water that would provide an escape from the crowded city. It was a conscious departure from the kinds of formal spaces that had typified the European gardens of earlier times.

Yet the designers knew that a park had to be used, and one intended popular use was for listening to music in a pastoral setting. So they devoted one section of their park to the Concert Grove, a formal space that would be even grander than Central Park's Mall. As they had done with architectural elements in Central Park, Olmsted and Vaux made the Lake visible from the Grove, but not vice versa; the island

and planted headlands cleverly disguised the formal space, making it unobtrusive when viewed from across the Lake.

Visitors to today's Concert Grove will find it much changed from Olmsted and Vaux's original vision. The original plan for this section of the park catered to 19th-century mores. A formal pedestrian concourse would be flanked by two viewing areas for horse carriages: one atop Breeze Hill, the other a Carriage Concourse between the grove and the East Drive. All these listening areas were arrayed in a broad curve, with its focus on Music Island, a small islet with a performance stage that had the broad sweep of the Lake as its stunning backdrop. Along the shore was also a space for listeners who would gather in rowboats or other waterborne conveyances, such as canoes.

Oriental Pavilion

Entering the grove from either the Willink or Lincoln Road entrances, or via the Cleft Ridge Span from the Lullwater, one comes upon a striking building with a broad hipped roof that seems far too heavy to be balanced as it is upon delicate cast-ductile-iron support columns. This is the Concert Grove Pavilion, another of Vaux's fine additions to the park. Designed and finished in 1874, the pavilion was immediately nicknamed the Oriental Pavilion for its Hindu-inspired architecture.

As majestic as the pavilion is, its role was originally to serve as an open-air seating area adjacent to

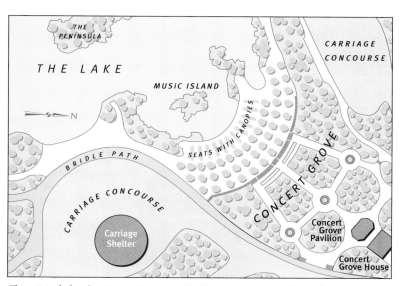

The original plan for Concert Grove provided for viewing of musical performances by both pedestrians and carriage riders. Vaux's planned Carriage Shelter was never built.

another Vaux-designed structure: the Concert Grove House. A probable collaboration with Thomas Wisedell (who did a lot of work with Vaux in the Concert Grove) this frame chalet housed a restaurant and comfort station. It survived until 1949, when it was unceremoniously demolished by Robert Moses, who also converted the Oriental Pavilion into a snack bar, with a brick enclosure built between its elegant columns. This would come to be a tragic addition, as on March 9, 1974, the refreshment stand caught fire. The flames quickly spread to the ornate roof, and the building was soon entirely engulfed, leaving little more than the iron support columns intact.

With the city's fiscal crisis then in full swing— the following year would see the famous *Daily News* headline "[President] Ford to City: Drop Dead"—the pavilion remained a fenced-in ruin until the 1980s, when it was restored complete with star-shaped stained-glass skylight, but this time without a snack bar. The restored pavilion is an excellent example of the Victorian style popular during Vaux's apprenticeship in

England, which borrowed heavily from Romanesque, Chinese, Moorish, and Egyptian motifs.

Sculpture in the Concert Grove

To the south of the pavilion, in the curving pathways and terraces that make up the Concert Grove proper, stands a collection of portrait busts of great composers including von Weber, Grieg, Mozart, and Beethoven. But the earliest bronze bust in this area was a singularly nonmusical one: the Washington Irving memorial just facing Concert Grove from across East Drive, which was donated to the city of Brooklyn in 1871 by the Honorable Demas Barnes, described in one account as a "patent medicine man who was elected to Congress."

The Irving memorial soon had company in the form of the busts contributed over the years by the United

Concert Grove has become home to various busts of famed musicians over the years, with Ludwig von Beethoven just one among the many composers represented.

Concert Grove Pavilion as it looked during the 19th century. The Oriental Pavilion, as it is sometimes called for its Chinese- and Moorish-influenced design, was completely restored after a 1974 fire, returning its hipped roof and 8-pointed, stained-glass skylight (above) to their original appearance.

German Singers of Brooklyn, who won them in national musical competitions and then donated them to the park. Some were also donated by the Norwegian Society. The Moore bust, however, was given by the St. Patrick Society of the City of Brooklyn on the 100th anniversary (1873) of his birth. As a historical footnote, observe that the inscriptions on the busts read "to the city of Brooklyn" for those erected before 1898, "to the borough of Brooklyn" for those thereafter, that year marking the consolidation of Manhattan, The Bronx, Brooklyn, Queens and Richmond Counties into greater New York City.

Statue of Abraham Lincoln

Beyond the busts stands a larger-than-life depiction of Abraham Lincoln, holding the Emancipation Proclamation and flanked by a pair of bronze eagles. (The eagles are replicas, replacing the originals stolen in the 1970s.) This statue, a gift from the War Fund Committee of Kings County, is one of the oldest in the park, dating to 1868; it originally stood in Grand Army Plaza, but was moved here in 1895 during one of the plaza's periodic remodelings.

The Lincoln statue's placement, in the dappled light of a grove of London plane trees, was originally intended to enable it to look out over the Lake, which with its Music Island was the focal point of the Concert Grove. But the music stand soon ran into problems: The acoustics proved inferior, even after an 1897 renovation, and the park's musical center was shifted to Music Grove, with Concert Grove renamed the Flower Garden.

Still, the area remained largely unchanged until 1960, when Parks Commissioner Moses had the Wollman Rink built at its southernmost edge.

Wollman Rink

To make room for the rink, Moses obliterated Music Island and its surrounding arm of water, leaving the Grove facing nothing more than a concrete skating slab. Lincoln now stares out over the chain-link fence surrounding the rink, looking for all the world as if he's consulting an original map of the site and wondering where the wonderful view has gone.

The rink itself, while arguably an eyesore, does provide 26,600 square feet of ice for skaters, as well as for the Brooklyn Blades amateur women's ice-hockey team. The Wollman Rink is open from November to March; call 718-287-6431 for hours of operation. There has been talk of relocating the rink to a portion of the current parking lot, but any decision is no doubt some time off.

Music in the Park

In 1925, controversy erupted in the neighborhoods surrounding Prospect Park. The problem: Noted bandleader Edwin Franko Goldman, whose free "people's concerts" in Central Park were a tremendous hit with the public, was balking at bringing them to the outer boroughs.

Evidently something changed his mind, because within a few years, Goldman's concerts had become a staple of summers in the park, drawing huge crowds on Tuesday and Saturday evenings. "Although he does not play jazz, Mr. Goldman is not adverse to the lighter classics by modern composers," noted the *Brooklyn Eagle*. In 1943, amid much fanfare, the composer proudly debuted a new march, "Hail, Brooklyn," which began: *In Prospect Park in Brooklyn/ Where we go to hear the band/ On summer evenings thrice each week/ A treat that's really grand...* It was a huge hit.

Throngs of Music Lovers

Music was always a part of Olmsted and Vaux's vision for a grand public park, and for it they designed Music Island, where performers could play to listeners arrayed across the Concert Grove. From the start, variety was the order of the day: An 1896 concert program for the Thirteenth Regiment Band opens with the "Star Spangled Banner," continuing with Theodore Mann's "Jolly Minstrels March," Rossini's "William Tell Overture," and a "popular selection"

including "Those Wedding Bells," "Rosey Posey," and "Benches in the Park," arranged for bells and xylophone solos, the effect of which can only be imagined.

Goldman in his day was among the elite of brass-band conductors and composers. (After famed bandleader and composer John Philip Sousa's death, his widow presented Goldman with her husband's baton). He began his Prospect Park performances in Concert Grove, but soon relocated to the Music Pagoda, where as many as 13,000 people would throng the Nethermead to hear his orchestra. The concerts continued without interruption for 4 decades (conducted by his son Richard Franko Goldman following Edwin's death in 1956), until dwindling popularity put an end to them in 1972.

Summer Celebration

While the Music Pagoda still sees occasional use by small groups, the two musical focal points of Prospect Park are now the Bandshell and Drummers' Grove, at opposite ends of the park's midsection. Each summer from June to September, the recently renovated Bandshell plays host to the Celebrate Brooklyn! festival, an eclectic mix of music, dance, film, and spoken-word performances spanning the breadth of the borough's diverse cultures. Recent years have seen such performers as Taj Mahal, Toshi Reagon, and the

The Lake

Skirting the edge of the skating rink, one finally comes upon the vista that was intended for patrons of Concert Grove: the view south across the Lake, the centerpiece of the park's southernmost section.

At 60 acres in expanse, the Prospect Park Lake is the largest lake in Brooklyn. (The competition isn't strong: It's also the borough's only lake.) Dug out with picks and shovels by an army of Olmsted's workers, it was originally sited not just for its scenic value but as an ice-skating locale. Each winter, local residents would watch for the red ball markers placed by parks workers at the entrances and on the trolley cars to indicate that it was open for skating; a turn-of-the-century *Brooklyn Eagle* headline boasted that "The Ice Is a Foot Thick and Solid Enough to Hold an Army of Brooklynites." But a gradually warming local climate, combined with plant growth that has warmed the water, made skating-thickness ice a thing of the past. There is still skating at the park, but now it is at the Wollman Rink.

The Lake's undulating shoreline and many bays and peninsulas—all originally carved out of undifferentiated Flatbush farmland—make it impossible to see the entire body of water at once, providing a classic Olmstedian sense of boundlessness. It also makes circumnavigating the lake a formidable task, so be prepared for a lengthy hike if you intend to traverse the entire shoreline.

Wildlife on and in the Lake

The Lake is also host to a profusion of wildlife, perched as it is on the Atlantic Flyway for migratory birds and offering abundant water and foliage. Waterfowl are a common site here as well, from mallard ducks and diving cormorants to a family of swans that has nested near the Park Circle entrance in recent years. Turtles are plentiful (several were transplanted from the Brooklyn Botanic Garden's Japanese Garden during its recent reconstruction), and can be seen sunning themselves on rocks and half-submerged tree limbs in the marshy channels that line the Lake.

The Lake teems with life beneath its surface as well, with thousands of largemouth bass that were stocked by the Parks Department many years ago for the dozens of anglers that gather daily on the shore for catch-and-release fishing. Since

Thousands of onlookers thronged the lakeshore to hear performances on a flag-bedecked Music Island. This scene is now the site of the Wollman Rink.

Alloy Orchestra's annual silent-film accompaniments. For a current schedule, contact Brooklyn Information and Culture at 718-855-7882, or at their website www.celebrate-brooklyn.org.

The other premier musical events in the park are the New York Philharmonic Orchestra's yearly summer visits and the every-other-year Metropolitan Opera's performances. Both are followed by a fireworks display.

While Celebrate Brooklyn! is Prospect Park's preeminent organized arts festival, the Drummers' Circle is something else altogether: a spontaneous gathering of drummers, dancers, and vendors of African descent that for over 25 years have been filling summer Sundays in the park with driving polyrhythms and joyous dance near the Ocean Avenue entrance. World-renowned musicians have been known to sit in on the weekly sessions, and several professional drumming and dance troupes have been born out of collaborations that began at the Drummers' Circle.

1946, each July, Macy's department store has sponsored a catch-and-release fishing contest for children 14 and under: Prizes are awarded every day for a week for the most and largest fish caught that day, and a special Grand Prize is awarded to whoever lands R. H. Macy*s, a large-mouth bass with silver tags released into the Lake at the start of the contest. Contact Prospect Park Alliance Special Events at 718-965-8969 for information.

Boating on the Lake

Perhaps the best way to experience the Lake is to get out on it, which can be done during the spring and summer months via the pedal-boat concession at Wollman Rink. Managed by the Prospect Park Alliance, these simple water conveyances replaced the traditional rowboats in the 1980s and have been an extremely popular attraction ever since. For hours and rates, call 718-282-7789; party rentals should call 718-965-6512.

The Honor Roll Memorial

On the lakeshore, beside the skating rink snack bar, is a granite wall bearing a set of bronze plaques and a central statue. This is the Brooklyn Honor Roll, commemorating the 2500 Brooklyn men and women who died in World War I—or as it was simply known at the time it was dedicated, the World War. Replacing a temporary wooden honor roll that had been erected during the war, it was designed by Arthur D. Pickering and sculpted by Augustus Lukeman in 1921. The central figure, a soldier accompanied by the Angel of Death,

stands among six bronze tablets bearing the names of the dead. Several of the panels have come loose and are now in storage with the Parks Department, awaiting restoration.

Originally standing on what was a peninsula jutting into the Lake, the Honor Roll is now firmly attached to the mainland by the bulk of the skating rink.

Walking south from the memorial, you will come upon a rustic shelter, a replacement for one of several that originally dotted the lakeshore during Olmsted and Vaux's day. (Four were placed on the Lake's eastern shore alone, to provide sunset views across the water.) The Lake was also the site of the Model Boat House, a 50-foot octagonal structure that in 1901 was built of park-grown locust and cedar wood to house model sailing ships on the park's eastern shore.

Unfortunately, none of the Lake's original shelters have survived into the present day. The Model Boat House burned down in 1956, and the other remaining rustic shelters were demolished around the same time. The shelter beside the Honor Roll, and a similar one facing it from the tip of the Peninsula, were installed in 1967, and a large five-sided shelter was restored to the Lake's east shore near the Parkside entrance in the fall of 2000.

Drummers' Grove

If your visit to the park falls on a Sunday after 2 p.m., you will, from the time you reached the Concert Grove, have heard the sound of percussive polyrhythms filling the air.

The Model Boathouse was built on the Lake's western shore in 1901 to house the miniature craft that had begun to boom in popularity. It burned down in 1956 and was not replaced.

The Lake, Brooklyn's largest body of fresh water, was created by Olmsted and Vaux out of 60 acres of Flatbush farmland. It is today a popular gathering place for birders, boaters, and fishers.

These are courtesy of the musicians playing at Drummers' Grove. For 30 years, a park tradition that has made its home in a small clearing just east of the Wollman Rink parking lot.

The Congo Square Drummers, named for the square in New Orleans where African slaves would go to play music while their owners were in church on Sundays, began in 1968 as an informal gathering of local musicians. "We couldn't play in our house, because our parents would kick us out," recalls Abiodun McCray, one of the group's founders and now a circle elder. "We had to have somewhere to rehearse, and just to play and rejoice." After playing at Jacob Riis Beach in the Rockaways and on the north Long Meadow, the drummers—just a handful then—soon settled on some benches near Prospect Park's Ocean Avenue entrance.

By the 1990s, the group had expanded into a renowned group that included dozens of drummers, dancers, and vendors, all congregating in the section of the park now officially renamed Drummers' Grove. While the world-class performers of the Congo Square Drummers make up the core of the weekly gatherings, the circle is open to all who respect its rules: no drinking, no smoking, no profanity, and respect for the performers and their ancestors. Flutes and other instruments can often be heard threading melodies amid the drumbeats. "As long as you can keep time, you can play," says McCray.

Accompanying the drummers are the dozens of dancers who fill the circle, and the 35 permitted vendors that line the path alongside. The marketplace's organizer, Agnes Free Spirit—"everyone just calls me Free Spirit"—first happened upon the circle more than 20 years ago, when she was walking her infant daughter through the park. "It was about two years before I even went in the circle to dance. And after that, I couldn't do no other dance. Because it's a very spiritual thing when you get in there. You feel the spirit."

New Shelter, Prospect Park, Brooklyn, N.Y.

Labeled the "New Shelter" in this turn-of-the-century postcard, the Peristyle was designed by Stanford White as a viewing station for the Parade Grounds to the south.

Along the Lake

Just to the south is another area that has undergone significant change since the park's early years. This was the site of Ford Bridge, a rustic span that crossed a small inlet that projected off the main body of the Lake just south of where the Rustic Shelter now stands. Alongside the bridge was a ford (hence the name), where riders on the bridle path could walk their steeds through the inlet for a refreshing dip in the water. Dammed and filled in 1916 to save on maintenance costs, the former inlet now serves as one of the park's barbecue zones, with several metal grills set up for picnickers.

Close by is also where, from 1987 to 1999, stood a tree trunk carved by local Haitian sculptor Deenps Bazile, representing the forest spirit; unfortunately, it has since been desecrated by vandals, leaving only the circle of logs known as the Gran Bwa around a shapeless central stump.

South of here, the undulating lakeshore makes for a maze of hidden inlets and narrow peninsulas,

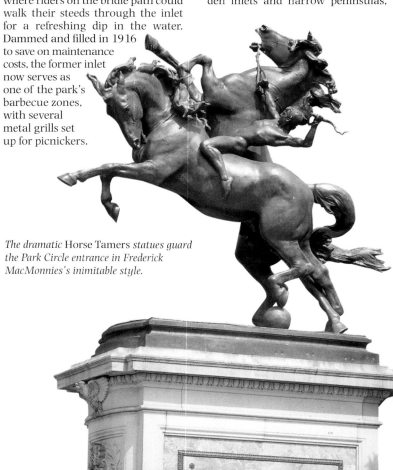

The dramatic Horse Tamers statues guard the Park Circle entrance in Frederick MacMonnies's inimitable style.

where turtles bask on sunken logs and anglers wait patiently for a strike. The scale of the lake is so vast, its meandering shore so intricate, that even on a day when it is crowded with fisherfolk, kids feeding (or chasing) the plentiful ducks and geese, and cyclists breezing along the straightaway of South Park Drive, there is still an overriding sense of isolation amidst nature.

The Pergola and the Peristyle

As the lake makes its graceful turn to the west along Parkside Avenue, it passes some of the more dramatic Beaux Arts additions to the park made at the turn of the century during the McKim, Mead & White era.

The first, at the park's southeasternmost entrance, is the designers' granite pergola, a pair of colonnades topped with wisteria-draped trellises that flank the path into the park.

A short distance to the west, wedged in between South Lake Drive and the park border, is the Peristyle, a dramatic classical structure that stands incongruously at the roadside. The limestone-and-terra-cotta pavilion was installed by McKim, Mead & White in 1903, replacing an earlier rustic shelter that stood on the site. Both served the same function: as a judging station for parades and military drills that once took place on the Parade Grounds across Parkside Avenue to the south.

Horse Tamers

Following the path east along the drive, you soon arrive at the Park Circle entrance, beside the traffic circle where Parkside Avenue, Coney Island Avenue, Prospect Park Southwest, and Fort Hamilton Parkway converge. Flanked by large hedges, the entrance is dominated by what is possibly sculptor Frederick MacMonnies's most memorable contribution to the park's architecture: The *Horse Tamers*, a pair of statues atop granite pedestals by Stanford White.

Sculpted in 1898 and dedicated in 1899, the work was first exhibited in 1900 at the Paris Exposition and in 1901 at the Pan-American Exposition in Buffalo. The daunting work was originally titled by its sculptor *The Triumph of Mind over Brute Force*. This Victorian sentiment is complicated, however, noted author M. M. Graff, when one notices that "Mind is not subduing the horse by any sort of intellectual persuasion but rather by lashing it over the head with a heavy braided quirt."

The Parade Grounds

Across Parkside Avenue stands a large green space that is part of the park but not part of the Landmark designation: the Parade Grounds.

When Olmsted and Vaux set about to design the park, they knew they would be required to provide space for military drills and sports,

The Parade Grounds in 1928. Though much redesigned over the last century and a half, it has always served as Brooklyn's main sports recreation area.

activities that they thought would hurt the plants and grass. Egbert Viele's original park proposal would have placed a parade ground in the East New York section of Brooklyn, several miles distant. Instead— much as they segregated libraries and museums to nearby "Institution Park" on the opposite side of Flatbush Avenue, now the site of the Brooklyn Botanic Garden—Olmsted and Vaux induced the city to purchase a rectangle of land to the south of the park for the exclusive use of militia groups, who could parade there to their hearts' content.

Military drills are no longer an important part of Brooklyn life, but the Parade Grounds remain one of the city's busiest athletic fields, with both children and adults packing its grounds to play baseball, softball, football, soccer, tennis, and innumerable other sports from dawn till dusk nearly year-round. Permit holders get precedence, and given the stiff competition for space, a permit is recommended during peak hours; call 718-965-6508 for information. The Parade Grounds are presently undergoing restoration that will be completed by 2004.

Wellhouse

North of the Park Circle entrance, at the northwest corner of the Lake, the shoreline skirts the base of Lookout Hill, the park's highest point. Along this runs Wellhouse Drive, a once heavily-used motorway that is now closed to traffic but links the East and West drives.

The Peninsula first presents visitors with an open meadow—a favorite of dog-walkers. Beyond lies a wooded area visited by many species of birds and waterfowl, including Canada geese that feed along the shoreline.

A short distance along this drive stands the small stone-and-brick structure that gives the drive its name. Designed by Vaux and built in 1869, the Wellhouse, constructed of bricks with walls 2 feet thick, housed a boiler and steam-driven machinery that was capable of raising 750,000 gallons of water a day. Pumped into a reservoir built into the west end of Lookout Hill, it then flowed out of a simulated spring at the base of Quaker Hill, down a gully, and into the Upper Pool, thereby feeding the park's entire water system. After the system was converted to city-supplied water in the early 20th century, making the well unnecessary, it was covered over. It remains, however, buried: a 70-foot deep hole, just 10 feet across at its top but broadening to 50 feet in diameter at its base. The Wellhouse itself is currently a maintenance facility, though there is talk of renovating it for use as a comfort station.

Peninsula

Opposite the Wellhouse, the Peninsula juts out into the Lake, providing one of the park's most isolated spots, and as such a haven for birds and birdwatchers. (Its meadow is also one of the park's open dog areas (see page 20), which can make for a difficult juxtaposition.) A dirt trail leads out to the shelter at the peninsula's tip, providing both a pleasant escape into wilderness and a lovely panoramic

view of the Lake's far shore.

On the north side of the Peninsula was originally to have stood a large building known as the Refectory. Described as resembling a well-appointed country inn, it was planned to be a sizable restaurant facing a set of broad terraces leading down to the water, much as Bethesda Terrace does in Central Park. The Refectory, however, fell victim to the Panic of 1873, which drained the Brooklyn city treasury, and by extension Olmsted and Vaux's construction budget. When the Refectory plan was abandoned, Wellhouse Drive was laid out through the site.

Just beyond the Wellhouse, before returning to the Nethermead, a stone obelisk stands at the base of Lookout Hill. This is the Maryland Monument, erected August 27, 1895, to memorialize how, as one contemporary account of the Battle of Brooklyn put it, "this gallant band, on that fateful morning, were cut to pieces." The monument itself is a slim granite shaft topped by a marble sphere, within decorative iron fence work. (For more on the ill-fated Maryland regiment, see the Battle of Brooklyn sidebar, page 62.)

Tour of Lookout and Quaker Hills

While Prospect Park's designers took pains to devise a space that would naturally draw visitors from point to point within it, two of the most prominent locations within the park stand relatively isolated. In one case, this is primarily an accident of geography; in the other, it is because the area in question is not technically part of the park at all.

Lookout Hill

Prospect Park, as we said, was named for Mount Prospect, the 200-foot-high hill that stood across Flatbush Avenue from the ultimate park site. The hill, now somewhat reduced in height, is presently occupied by the considerably smaller Mount Prospect Park.

At the time of Prospect Park's creation, its most dramatic vistas came from Lookout Hill, the section of the glacial moraine that towers above

the flat outwash plain below. According to 19th-century accounts, visitors could spy the Atlantic Ocean, four miles distant, from the peak of Lookout Hill, with a similar vantage westward offering views as far as the harbor and New Jersey beyond.

This spectacular outlook was to be the centerpiece of the park in Olmsted and Vaux's design, with all paths ultimately converging on this central peak. They planned to adorn it with a 300-foot-long oval carriage court, along with a refreshment pavilion and a "terraced platform one hundred feet in length, with seats and awnings." At the summit, alongside the reservoir that fed the park's water system, would stand a tall stone observation tower, from which visitors could have a panoramic view of Brooklyn and beyond.

Aside from the carriage court, none of these planned additions were ever built. The top of Lookout Hill may be reached by steep climbs up stone steps from several access points along Well House and Center Drives. It is now a quiet, largely overgrown meadow surrounded by such invasive trees as Norway and sycamore maples. Smog and foliage have conspired to reduce the view somewhat, but on a clear day in win-

The Maryland Monument stands at the base of Lookout Hill, in memory of those killed at the Battle of Brooklyn.

ter one can still see much of surrounding Brooklyn.

As a relatively low-trafficked area of the park, Lookout Hill has also become a haven for birds and wildlife, and is a favorite destination of bird-watchers as well. The one-time carriage court has been converted into a grassy field where wildflowers are being planted to attract butterflies and other insects. This "butterfly meadow" is ablaze with insect-friendly flowers and plants, including the aromatic butterfly bush with its striking purple flowers.

The slopes of Lookout Hill have been badly eroded in recent years as a result of increased foot and bicycle traffic. (Mountain bikers, in particular, have devastated several sections of hillside). Park staff and volunteers are in the process of shoring up the hillside with water bars and protective netting, which can be seen in particular on the slope leading down to Well House Drive and the Lake.

Quaker Hill

To the north and west of Lookout Hill is another large section of moraine—at its highest point just a few feet shorter than its neighbor.

This is Quaker Hill, so named for the cemetery run by the pacifist abolitionist sect whose members were instrumental in establishing religious freedom in colonial times.

The Friends Cemetery, as it is also referred to, was first established in 1849, though burials had been taking place there since at least the 1820s on the rocky, unfarmable terminal moraine. Occupying the low rise between Lookout Hill and the Long Meadow ball fields, the cemetery is not actually part of the park, remaining in private hands since the park was built around it in the 1860s.

Originally a long rectangle running from Ninth to Fourteenth streets, the cemetery was reduced in size to a nearly square plot delineated by the former routes of Eleventh and Fourteenth streets, between Eleventh and Twelfth avenues (both thoroughfares now reduced to stubs by the intervening park). Quakers were assured direct passage there from the Sixteenth Street entrance.

Though the cemetery is closed to the public, parkgoers can catch glimpses through the fence of the simple grave markers, used for all those interred regardless of wealth as part of Quaker tradition. Among the better-known names buried here are Raymond Ingersoll, the city official for whom the Ingersoll Library is named, the Mott family of apple juice fame, and Montgomery Clift, the noted actor who was born to Quaker parents.

Willink Tour

When the park's Willink Entrance was first sketched out by Olmsted and Vaux, it was a concession to the inevitability of change. Although much of the surrounding land was mostly vacant at the time, they were certain that the city's inexorable growth, further spurred by the proximity of the park, would soon prompt new development along the park's rural fringes. And while it took a few decades, they were, of course, correct: The neighboring areas of Crown Heights, Prospect-Lefferts Gardens, and Flatbush boomed throughout the 20th century, first with Jewish immigrants who followed the subway lines to new developments in central Brooklyn, and more recently with the arrival of immigrants from the English- and French-speaking Caribbean. The Willink Entrance, once the park's back door, soon became one of the most used access point to the park.

Most visitors to the Willink Entrance will come through the intersection of Flatbush and Ocean avenues and Empire Boulevard, a traffic-clogged corner that requires some care to navigate as a pedestrian. If traveling on the D or Q trains to the Prospect Park stop, keep a careful eye out for cars turning from Flatbush as you cross Ocean Avenue to the park. While unremarkable now, this unassuming corner was once the scene of one of Brooklyn's greatest disasters.

On November 1, 1918, workers at the Brooklyn Rapid Transit company went on strike to protest the dismissal of 29 motormen for unionizing. To break the strike, the company pressed managers and supervisors into service driving its trains. One, a 23-year-old dispatcher named Edward Luciano, ill with Spanish influenza, took the S-curve into the Malbone Street tunnel at far too great a speed. The first three cars jumped the tracks, their wooden panels "crumbling like fruit cases," according to one contemporary account. Ninety-three people died, and the Malbone Avenue Disaster became so infamous that the street's name was later changed to Empire Boulevard.

Another famous Brooklyn catastrophe struck a few blocks away and 40 years later, when the Brooklyn Dodgers abandoned their native borough for the riches of Los Angeles. Ebbets Field (1913-1957), which had been the emotional heart of the borough through years of heartache and occasional triumph, was torn down soon after and replaced by the Ebbets Field houses, visible as the drab brown housing complex that peers up from behind the Botanic Garden.

The Willink Entrance is fairly typical of the several Beaux Arts entrances designed for the park by McKim, Mead & White during the opening years of the 19th century. Stone benches curve around an exceptionally broad cobblestone plaza, as a pair of granite pillars stand watch.

Entering the park on the leftmost path from the Willink Entrance, you pass on your left a yellow brick building with stone columns and a red tile roof. This is the Willink Entrance Comfort Station, recently restored by the Prospect Park Alliance, with informational signs added about the park and its history.

The Carousel

If you turn right and cross the park drive entrance, you'll find yourself at the restored Carousel, an octagonal structure of red and white brick containing 51 carved wooden horses as well as a lion, a giraffe, a deer, and two chariots adorned with fire-breathing dragons. Originally built in 1951 to take the place of the carousel near the Picnic House that had burned down 16 years earlier, the Carousel was actually a composite of two Coney Island carousels built by renowned Brooklyn designer Charles Carmel, one dating from 1915, the other 1918. The current carousel represents one of the few remaining Carmel designs still in existence.

In the 1980s, the Carousel was given a complete overhaul courtesy of the Prospect Park Alliance, its fading horses hand-stripped and repainted in their original colors by Will Morton VIII, a Denver sculptor and nationally acclaimed carousel restoration expert. Because the nearby zoo was closed for construction, the horses were stored in the zoo's zebra house while Morton did his restoration work. A *New Yorker* reporter who visited the sculptor there noted that Morton "answered the door of the zebra house with the sobriety of a doctor whose patients are very very sick."

The Carousel is open for rides on weekends and holiday afternoons from April to October. Rides are just 50 cents each, and there is wheelchair accessibility. It's also possible to rent out the Carousel for private parties; call 718-965-6512 for information.

East Wood Arch and Flatbush Turnpike Tollbooth

If you veer left, away from the Carousel, you'll find yourself following a wooded path between two towering tulip trees. This path leads to the East Wood Arch, along with Endale Arch one of the first two designed for the park by Vaux, in 1867. It shares with Endale the pointed arch and banded stonework testifying to its Syrio-Egyptian influences, but doesn't frame quite such a dramatic vista. The path continues beyond a few hundred feet before arriving back at the head of the Lullwater, near Binnen Falls or, turning left, at the Boathouse.

If instead you turn right, heading toward the front of the Carousel, you come across a small wooden structure that is easily overlooked by the

The Prospect Park carousel was built in 1951, but its component parts are far older, dating from a pair of Coney Island carousels designed in the early 20th century. Inset: The rondos around the top of the carousel are modern depictions based on historic photos of well-known areas in the park.

Lefferts Homestead, the park's oldest building, offers a variety of programming for children that focuses on Brooklyn's history and the groups that have lived here.

park visitor. There's little to mark that it is in fact one of the oldest structures in the park: the Flatbush tollbooth. Built in the 1850s by the Brooklyn, Flatbush and Jamaica Plank Road Company for the taking of tolls along then new Flatbush Avenue, it stood on the west side of the street between Winthrop and Fenimore when the park was built. (This is roughly opposite today's Drummers' Grove, one block away from the park.)

When the Flatbush Road Company went out of business in 1893, the booth was transferred as a gift to the last Flatbush Road commissioner, John Moore, who placed it in his backyard on Tilden Avenue in East Flatbush. Rediscovered 32 years later, it was again relocated, this time to the park—in the general vicinity of its original home, at least. Restored in recent years as an information center and gift shop, it is open every weekend.

Lefferts Homestead Children's Historic House Museum

Behind the tollbooth, at the end of a narrow dirt path leading to a small wooden gate, is the oldest building in the park, and one of the oldest in the city: the Lefferts Homestead. It was built in 1777 by Dutch farmer Peter Lefferts after his previous house was burned by American soldiers 3 days before the Battle of Long Island. With its large rooms and dormer windows, it is a handsome example of farmhouse living for the well-to-do of that era. In 1918, the Lefferts family moved out, deeding the house to the city, and the dwelling was moved from its original site on the east side of Flatbush between Maple and Midwood to the park.

The Lefferts Homestead is currently run by the Prospect Park Alliance as a children's museum, dedicated to teaching kids about life in the 1820s and '30s, not just life for the Dutch family that owned the property, but for their Lenape Indian neighbors and their African slaves and later employees as well. (New York was a large slave-owning state during the late 18th century, and Kings County, with its many farms, had the most slaves of the five counties around New York City.) Exhibits include a replica Lenape child's bed, lined with deerskin, and a re-created

Domestic
Animals

Animals in Our Lives

Baboons

Animal
Lifestyles

Aviary

Bald Eagle

Sea Lions

Prairie
Dogs

World of Animals

Porcupine

Red Panda

Nests

Entran

DISCOVERY

Ostrich

TRAIL

Wallaby

Entrance

FLATBUSH AVENUE

Carousel

Lefferts
Homestead

same day, the nearby zoo's sheep are sheared, and the wool brought to the Homestead for spinning. The flax, an important crop for making clothing in colonial times, is harvested in August, and made into linen in the fall. Harvest Fest, in September, and Winter Fest, after Thanksgiving, are other popular events, as is Pinkster Day, a re-creation of a Dutch and African American celebration of spring that was widely celebrated in the colonial era.

The two-story museum contains seven rooms, although there are other rooms in the farmhouse that are not part of the museum. Two rooms, an upstairs bedroom and a downstairs parlor, are restored to their colonial appearance. For information, call 718-789-2822.

Prospect Park Zoo

To the north of Lefferts Homestead, behind a sturdy iron fence, is the Prospect Park Zoo. Originally the site of the Deer Paddock, where deer wandered free in a meadow slightly removed from the park paths, and later occupied by a small meadow and the Wild Fowl Pond, this area was transformed in the 1930s when Robert Moses chose it as the new site for the park's zoo, replacing the Menagerie that then stood near the top of Sullivan Hill. Here, Works Progress Administration workers built a half circle of brick buildings, designed by Central Park Zoo architect Aymar Embury II. Bas reliefs on the zoo buildings depict scenes from Rudyard Kipling's *Jungle Books.*

African child's bed, made of rope and straw.

The Homestead also offers a variety of games and storytelling for children (its annual "Mystery of History Game," in which kids ferret out the clues to historical questions while learning research skills, is especially popular), as well as a full season of post colonial-style gardening. The crop year begins with Linsey-Woolsy Weekend in the spring, when flax is planted; on the

Opposite page: The barks of cavorting sea lions have been known to startle bus riders on nearby Flatbush Avenue. Above: On the zoo's Discovery Trail, children can visit with prairie dogs in their own "burrows."

A Snowy Owl stares down visitors with its predatory gaze.

A smaller relative of the kangaroo, the Parma Wallaby (above) dines on grasses and herbs, and can often be seen relaxing in its grassy enclosure. At left, a tiny Tree Nymph frog rests upon a half-submerged leaf.

The largest member of the rodent family, the capybara's size belies its placid, non-aggressive character. The name capybara means "master of the grasses" in Guarani, one of the languages indigenous to its South American habitat.

The zoo's Hamadryas baboons, natives of northern Africa and the Arabian Peninsula, go about their complex social lives before the eyes of zoo onlookers. On June 1, 2000, the zoo's baboon troop welcomed its first new addition, when a baby was born to mother Matara and father Simen.

The tiny Cotton-top Tamarin (left) can leap easily from branch to branch in search of food. A Red Panda (above) bears a striking facial resemblance to the unrelated raccoon. Below, a Bald Eagle obligingly spreads its wings for patriotic zoo visitors.

Meerkats, relatives of the mongoose, have been called the "Solar Panel of the Animal World" for their ability to warm themselves with solar radiation. Their dark eye markings also act as natural sunglasses.

After many years of dilapidation and complaints about mistreatment of animals, the zoo got a complete overhaul in 1993. It is now dedicated to exhibits geared toward teaching children about animals and their natural habitats, and operated by the Wildlife Conservation Society, which also runs the Bronx and Central Park zoos. (Individual or family memberships to the WCS gain entrance to all its facilities; call 718-220-5111 for membership information or join online at www.wcs.org/home/43/480/4283.) One of the first additions one notices is on the path from the main entrance, where a set of fantastic oversize steel sculptures have been installed, depicting a chameleon, a frog being devoured by a snake, fish heads, and finally a tremendous octopus that straddles the path.

The World of Animals

The first building, the World of Animals, leads to the center's Discovery Trail, a selection of live animals shown in reproductions of their native habitats, along with interactive exhibits. Prairie dogs are accompanied by a "burrow" that children can climb into themselves, while a pond stocked with turtles and fish features metal "lily pads" that kids can walk on. Other animals here include wallabies (small relatives of the kangaroo), a pair of emus, a red panda, and giant capybara. The animals often ensconce themselves deep in the foliage, especially in hot weather, so be patient and bring binoculars if visiting on a sunny summer afternoon. (A child-height telescope is also available for better viewing of the wallaby enclosure.)

Animal Lifestyles

In the Animal Lifestyles building, one will find a variety of small animals, ranging from mundane creatures like frogs, turtles, and birds to such exotic creatures as blind cave fish and Cape Rock hyrax, large guinea-pig-like rodents native to southern Africa. This building also contains the viewing room for one of the zoo's largest and most popular exhibits: its Hamadryas baboons, large monkeys with brown-speckled pelts and dramatic bright pink rumps. In June 2000, a baby baboon was born to the pack, delighting park visitors.

Animals in Our Lives

The third and final building is Animals in Our Lives, which contains everyday animals you might not expect in a zoo: gerbils, chickens, pigeons, and such aquarium fish as tetras and platys. The exhibits are designed to give children an appreciation of these animals and their role in human society: the chicken exhibit, for example, contains a red jungle fowl of the type from which domestic chickens were first bred. Behind this building is an enclosure with barnyard animals such as sheep and goats.

The zoo's centerpiece is its oval sea lion pool, where these playful sea mammals cavort in the water and sunbathe on land, emitting loud barks that have been known to surprise bus riders on nearby Flatbush Avenue. Feedings are three times daily; call for the current times.

The Prospect Park Zoo is open 365 days a year, with children under 3 admitted free. (All children 16 and under must be accompanied by an adult.) For hours or other information, call 718-399-7339.

"Lioness and Cubs" Statue

The Zoo's Flatbush Avenue entrance is opposite the main exhibit buildings: a pair of curved brick staircases that descend the steep earthen wall created when the avenue was raised on a causeway in the mid-19th century. At the base of the stairs is a statue of a lioness with her cubs, sculpted by Victor Peters in 1899, which has a long and contro-

The Emerald Tree Boa is born a terracotta orange-red, then gradually assumes its brilliant green color over its first few months of life.

versial history in the park. Originally sited at the Park Circle entrance it was later moved to the Concert Grove. There it soon became popular with local kids, who liked to slide down the lioness's smooth bronze back.

This routine lasted until 1934, when newly appointed Parks Commissioner Robert Moses had a five-foot wire fence erected around the statue, saying it had been "mutilated." As the only notable change to the statue was a slight polishing of its upper surface by generations of juvenile behinds, local parents were outraged. "It shows what happens when we let Manhattan run Brooklyn," fumed one mother to the *Brooklyn Eagle,* while another parent asked sarcastically, "What are they going to do, charge kids a quarter to slide down?"

The statue was out on a pedestal on the drive outside of the zoo in 1949. In the early 1990s it was moved to its present location: behind a holly hedge, protected from molestation by tiny bushes.

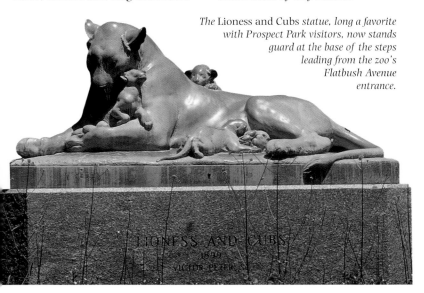

The Lioness and Cubs *statue, long a favorite with Prospect Park visitors, now stands guard at the base of the steps leading from the zoo's Flatbush Avenue entrance.*

SPORTS IN THE PARK

Bicycling

Bicycling has been one of the most popular pastimes in Prospect Park since its opening. In the 1890s, one observer called Brooklyn "one of the greatest wheelman's cities in the country," and a summer Sunday in the park will do nothing to convince one that that assessment has changed.

It wasn't until 1974 that park drives were first closed to traffic on weekends and parts of each weekday. The use of the park roads soon became wildly popular among the borough's cyclists and joggers. The following times are currently designated car-free: Weekends, All Year: Friday, 7 p.m. to Monday, 6 a.m.; Holidays, All Year: 7 p.m. prior to holiday until 6 a.m. the following day; Summer Weekdays [April to November]: 9 a.m.-5 p.m and 7 p.m-10 p.m; The winter schedule will probably be the same but at the time of publication remains undecided.

During hours that the drives are open to auto traffic, cyclists must stay in the lane designated for bicycles. The rest of the day, all of the drives are open to bicycle traffic—except East Lake Drive at the Parkside and Ocean Avenue entrance near Wollman Rink, where cars are allowed in at all times. While motorists are asked to drive cautiously in this part of the drive, it's always a good idea to use care here, remaining in the bicycle lane and alert for auto traffic. At all times, skaters and cyclists must obey car rules, and faster riders are to remain in the outside (rightmost) lanes when drives are open to bikes and other recreational use.

Riding bikes on pedestrian paths or off-road is expressly forbidden. The park ecosystems have been ravaged in recent years by compaction of soil and destruction of undergrowth by mountain bikes, and only if riders keep to the paved roadways can they be allowed to recover.

Running and Rollerblading

Runners and inline skaters are welcome in Prospect Park, both on paved paths and on the park drives, where a separate lane has been allocated to runners, alongside the bike

.92 miles
1.48 kilometers

.57 miles
.92 kilometers

.23 miles
.37 kilometers

.77 miles
1.24 kilometers

1.14 miles
1.83 kilometers

.62 miles
1.00 kilometer

.62 miles
1.00 kilometer

.60 miles
.97 kilometers

Baseball and Softball

There are seven ball fields for baseball and softball in Long Meadow, and another six in the Parade Grounds. Little League games in the park are coordinated by Prospect Park Baseball. For more information, call Prospect Park Baseball at 718-965-3741.

In addition, the permit office at Litchfield Villa issues permits for organized games in the park and Parade Grounds each year. Call 718-965-6508 for permit info.

Tennis

Prospect Park's tennis facilities are located in the Parade Grounds, across Parkside Avenue to the south of the park proper. Tennis permits are $5 for single play, while season permits are $50 for adults, $20 for seniors, and $10 for children, and can be obtained at Litchfield Villa from April through October; at other times, visit the Parade Grounds tennis courts for permits.

Ice Skating

Wollman Rink provides 26,600 square feet of ice for skaters, as well as for the Brooklyn Blades amateur women's ice-hockey team. Open from November to March, call 718-287-6431 for hours of operation.

lane. (See Bicycling section, above, for hours when the park is closed entirely to traffic.) A complete circuit of the circular park drive is 3.35 miles; the perimeter of the park, if you stick to the sidewalks outside it, is 4.35 miles. For more information on running and races in Prospect Park, contact the New York Road Runners Club at 212-860-4455; the Brooklyn Road Runners Club at 718-259-1481; or the Prospect Park Track Club at 718-595-2049.

Pedal Boats

From mid-May through Columbus Day, pedal boats are available for rental at the Wollman Rink from Thursday through Sunday, plus holidays. For $10 an hour plus a $10 refundable deposit, groups can propel themselves across the Lake, exploring all its hidden bays and inlets. For more information about pedal boat rentals, call 718-282-7789; for pedal boat party rentals, call 718-965-6512. In 2002 a touring boat powered by electricity will leave the Boathouse for tours of the waterway for up to 15 people.

Horseback Riding

The Park bridle path runs from Park Circle to the southwest corner of the Long Meadow, with an additional path circling the Lake and entering the Ravine. Horses may be rented for $20 an hour from the nearby Kensington Stables; call 718-972-4588 to make a reservation, or visit www.kensingtonstables.com for more information.

1.16 miles
1.87 kilometers

.77 miles
1.24 kilometers

.71 miles
1.14 kilometers

.12 miles
.19 kilometers

• • • • • • • • • • • •
Bridle Path

WILDLIFE IN THE PARK

Prospect Park is a respite of greenery and waterways not just for Brooklyn's human residents but for its birds as well, with hundreds of species either residing there or stopping by on their way along the Atlantic migratory flyway. (New York City is actually a convergence point for two main flyways, with some species coming down the Hudson River from Canada and the Adirondacks, and others following the glacial moraine down the New England coast.) Recent years have seen a huge resurgence in small birds like sparrows, warblers, and flickers, which come in large masses to feed on the park's ample food supply—as well as hawks and eagles that feed on the smaller birds. Bird-watchers in the winter will often spot as many as 60 species in a single day, while sightings during migration season can number more than 100. The Brooklyn Bird Club is currently compiling a database of bird sightings, which it plans to link to the new Audubon Center in the Boathouse.

Among the best bird-watching sites in the park are its more isolated, overgrown areas, such as the Peninsula, the Lullwater, the Midwood, the Vale of Cashmere, and especially the slopes of Lookout Hill, where recent avian visitors have included such rarities as a barred owl. Ducks, herons, cormorants, and other waterfowl are frequent denizens of the park's waterways— one flock of mallards has taken to wintering in the park, content to be fed by park visitors in the colder months.

In addition to birds, a startling variety of wildlife makes its permanent or temporary home among the fields, ponds, and forests of Prospect Park. Squirrels are ubiquitous, while chipmunks are plentiful among the underbrush of the Midwood and on the slopes of Breeze Hill, while a colony of cottontail rabbits has taken up residence near the Zoo.

The park also supports a growing population of bats, aided by the recovery of the park's ecosystem and by several "bat boxes" installed by parks workers (one pair is clearly visible on a dead tree near the head of the Ambergill). Butterflies have returned in droves to the newly planted meadows, particularly one on the top of Lookout Hill that is being planted with flowers that attract butterflies and bees. Local nature lovers are cautiously hopeful that this wildlife will survive the pesticide spraying to contain the West Nile virus that the city instituted in 1999 and 2000.

Female

Male

Wood Duck
Aix sponsa
17 - 20 in. long

Female

Green-winged Teal
Anas crecca
13 - 16 in. long

Male

Ruddy Duck
Oxyura jamaicensis
14 - 16 in. long

Male

Female

Canvasback
Aythya valisineria
19 - 24 in. long

Herring Gull
Larus argentatus
22 - 26 in. long

Great Egret
Casmerodius albus
37 - 41 in. long

Black-crowned Night-Heron
Nycticorax nycticorax
23 - 28 in. long

Double-crested Cormorant
Phalacrocorax auritus
29 - 36 in. long

Female

Male

Male

American Black Duck
Anas rubripes
21 - 25 in. long

Bufflehead
Bucephala albeola
13 - 16 in. long

Female

Male

Mallard
Anas platyrynchos
20 - 28 in. long

American Crow
Corvus brachyrynchos
17-21 in. long

European Starling
Sturnus vulgaris
7 - 8 1/2 in. long

Common Grackle
Quiscalus quiscul
10-12 1/2 in. long

Blue Jay
Cyanocitta cristata
11-12 1/2 in. long

Northern Mockingbird
Mimus polyglotto
9 -11 in. long

Downy Woodpecker
Picoides pubescens
6 - 7 in. long

Male

Female

Male

Female

House Finch
Carpodacus mexicanus
5 - 5 1/2 in. long

Female

Male

Song Sparrow
Melospiza melodia
5 - 7 in. long

House Sparrow
Passer domesticus
5 - 6 in. long

Female

Yellow Warbler
Dendroica petechia
4 1/2 - 5 1/2 in. long

Male

Golden-crowned Kinglet
Regulus satrapa
3 1/4 - 4 1/4 in. long

Red-tailed Hawk
Buteo jamaicensis
19-26 in. long

Red-winged Blackbird
Agelaius phoeniceus
7 - 9 1/2 in. long

Male

Male

Female

Northern Cardinal
Cardinalis cardinalis
7 1/2 - 8 1/2 in. long

Female

Mourning Dove
Zenaida macroura
10 - 12 in. long

American Robin
Turdus migratorius
9 - 11 in. long

97

TREES IN THE PARK

When Prospect Park was carved from the hills and swampland of 19th-century rural Brooklyn, the forest that existed there was of a kind that once covered most of America, from eastern Massachusetts to eastern Texas. It was the type now known to scientists as an oak-hickory-chestnut forest, for its three most prominent trees, all of which were prominent in Olmsted and Vaux creations, along with such other canopy trees as maples, elms, and tulip trees.

All that began to change in 1904, when botanists at the Bronx Zoo discovered that their chestnut trees were beginning to die. A fungus called *Cryphonectria parasitica*, traveling from China in a shipment of nursery trees, had infected the zoo's many towering chestnuts; within two years, the disease had spread as far as Virginia.

It was the beginning of the Great Chestnut Blight. The American chestnut population, with no native resistance to the alien fungus, was quickly overrun. By 1909, every chestnut in Prospect Park had succumbed, and by mid-century not a single mature specimen remained on the entire continent. Only the roots of some trees survived, periodically sending up shoots that would die off before reaching 20 feet in height. The American chestnut, once a commonplace sight in the continent's forests, now survives only as a scrubby understory tree.

A survey of the trees along Prospect Park's walks and open areas in the 1990s revealed that the most common tree species were black cherry, Norway maple, sycamore maple, red oak, ash, elm, sweet gum, pin oak, London plane, and eastern white pine. Of these, the Norway maple and sycamore maple are both introduced and have pushed out native trees. The many oaks, ashes, cherries, and sweet gums, however, are a reminder of the forest that once grew here, and that in many ways still does grow here, if a bit modified by time and a changing ecosystem.

Among the more notable trees in the park:

Oak: Oaks are among the most common trees in the park, having proved resistant to the diseases that have ravaged other native hardwoods. (They are also among the longest-lived: oaks in the park have been dated to the 17th century, and some oaks have been known to live 600 years.) Varieties include the red oak (broad, many-pointed leaves), white oak (more rounded leaves with whitish undersides), pin oak (many-pointed leaves with deep indentations), and turkey oak (leaves with narrow, single-pointed lobes). A branch of the beech family, the oaks are a "masting" species, meaning they may go several years without producing many acorns, then let loose with a crop of as many as 7000 acorns on a single tree. These acorns are eagerly gobbled up by the park's many squirrels, which have learned to selectively store the different species: red oak acorns, which sprout later in the year, are buried, while the more perishable white oak acorns are eaten immediately.

Sweet gum and sour gum: These two species are common to the Northeast and flourish in damp lowlands. The sweet gum is immediately recognizable from its star-shaped leaves and spiky seedballs. Both sweet gums and sour gums are found throughout the park, particularly around the Pools. An especially large sour gum (or black tupelo, the alternate name by which its Parks Department label marks it) stands on the Long Meadow just west of Roosevelt Hill.

Black cherry: Unlike the flowering cherry, imported from Japan in 1912, the black cherry is native to this region. The small, bitter fruit, appearing in late summer, can be made into cough syrup, wine, and jelly, and provides a feast for migrating birds every fall. A visit to the slopes of Lookout Hill in October will often turn up flocks of robins nested in the many black cherry trees, getting tipsy off the berries, which by then have fermented on the branch.

American elm: The profile of an American elm is unmistakable from a distance: the tall, straight trunk, gradually branching near the top and topped by a broad, symmetrical crown of spreading leaves. From up close, its serrated leaves are just as distinctive, as are the tiny whitish flowers it lets loose in the spring. Dutch elm disease has killed many of Prospect Park's specimens, with the best surviving ones scattered around

Long Meadow, along with one spectacular grove that survives on a small knoll near the Pools.

Linden: Also called the American Basswood, the linden is one of the most common trees along Prospect Park's meadows, with many large specimens along the east side of Long Meadow and in the Nethermead. Lindens are immediately recognizable for their heart-shaped leaves, and slender, leaflike bracts that in early summer produce a profusion of yellowish flowers with a sweet, perfumey scent.

Beech: The two types of beech in the park, American and European beech, are easily recognized by their smooth gray bark; they can be distinguished by their leaves, which are papery and toothed on the American variety, glossy and purplish on the European. Their distinctive fuzzy beechnuts not only gave their name to a type of gum but were the primary food source for the huge flocks of passenger pigeons that once covered eastern North America before their extinction at the hands of humans in the early 20th century. Beeches grow to a height of 80 feet and are second only to oaks in longevity among locally native trees, living for as long as 360 years.

Maples: Though its cousin the Norway maple is an imported invasive, red maples are indigenous to New York's ecosystem. Unique among trees in being able to thrive in both dry or swampy soil, its five-pointed leaves—with three prominent lobes topping a pair of smaller lobes at the leaf base—turn brilliant crimson in fall; add in the tree's tiny red flowers in spring and reddish wingnut-shaped seeds, and its name is well-earned. Sugar maples, the tree

tapped for their syrup across New England, look similar to red maples during the summer, then turn fiery orange in autumn. Maples, while not a major canopy tree, are excellent at biding their time, capable of growing slowly in the shaded understory for as long as 150 years, then shooting up once a fallen tree opens a gap in the canopy above.

Tulip tree: The tulip tree can grow to heights of well over 100 feet, with a straight trunk that can rise more than half the tree's height before branching off. This is an adaptation made necessary by the tree's lack of shade tolerance: the tulip tree grows fast, racing to find space amid the tight forest canopy, then retains only its sunlit topmost branches. It's often hard to identify tulip trees from the ground for this reason, but if you carefully scan the forest canopy or find a young specimen, you can spot its distinctive leaves in the shape of a tulip silhouette, and its yellow-orange flowers in the spring. In the fall, its large bright yellow leaves coat the ground, earning the tulip tree its other name, the yellow poplar.

Other trees in Prospect Park include: **black walnuts**, with their paired rows of leaves and dangling catkins, which produce a chemical that dissuades other trees from growing nearby; **hawthorns**, with their multi-serrated leaves and bright red fruits in the fall, found especially at the north end of Long Meadow; **sassafras**, a shrubby tree with oblong leaves of one, two, or three lobes, and roots that were used in early America to make the beverage known as sarsaparilla; and **birches**, both the well-known paper birch with its peeling bark, and the dark-gray black birch, whose twigs contain wintergreen oil and are the main ingredient in birch beer.

BROOKLYN
BOTANIC
GARDEN

ENJOYING THE GARDEN

Rules and Regulations

The Brooklyn Botanic Garden is a greenscape, but it is not a park. It is, in fact, a living museum. To maintain both the natural beauty and the educational experience and to protect the plant collections, the garden enforces certain rules and regulations for visitors:

The only food and beverages allowed in the garden are available for purchase at the Terrace Cafe. The only exceptions are bottled water and baby bottles.

Sitting on lawns, with the exception of the Cherry Esplanade, is not permitted, and blankets and folding chairs are not allowed in the garden at all.

To avoid damaging the plantings, do not pick flowers, walk in flower beds, or climb trees.

Children must remain under adult supervision at all times.

Pets are not permitted in the garden.

Radios and other audio devices may be used with earphones only.

Shirts and shoes are required.

No athletic activities, including ball playing, Frisbee tossing, biking, skating, rollerblading, jogging, or kite flying, are allowed in the garden.

Personal photography is allowed, but commercial photography is permitted only by prior arrangement. Tripods or easels may not be set up in the Conservatory, the Japanese garden, flower beds, or in such a way as to block any outdoor paths.

Hours of Operation

April-September: Tuesday-Friday, 8 a.m.-6 p.m.; weekends and holidays: 10 a.m.-6 p.m.
October-March: Tuesday-Friday, 8 a.m.-4:30 p.m; weekends and holidays: 10 a.m.-4:30 p.m.
The Steinhardt Conservatory always opens at 10 a.m. and always closes one half hour before the garden closes.

Admission Fees and Garden Membership

The Brooklyn Botanic Garden has an admission fee: $5 per adult and $3 for seniors and students.

Children 15 and under are free. The garden is open free of charge Tuesdays and Saturday mornings until noon.

For frequent garden visitors, another way to save money and support the garden is to become a garden member, which gives you free admission, discounts at the Garden Gift Shop, classes and tours, entry to special members-only summer evening hours, and more. Another benefit is receiving four quarterly publications on gardening produced by the garden—the 21st Century Gardening Series handbooks. For information about becoming a member, call 718-623-7210 or visit the garden website at www.bbg.org.

Guided Tours of the Garden

Led by volunteer garden guides, tours are available for free on Saturday and Sunday afternoons (except on major holiday weekends) at 1 p.m., leaving from the Visitor Center. To arrange group tours, call 718-623-7220. And, of course, there are always the garden's curators, who can often be found in their dark green uniforms tending their plants and answering the questions of inquisitive visitors.

Events and Ongoing Programs

In addition to its ongoing mission of displaying plants in an educational and aesthetic environment, the Brooklyn Botanic Garden also runs a variety of programs and special events for adults and children alike. The most well-known are the special festivals scattered throughout the year, from the Sakura Matsuri cherry blossom festival in late April to the

Chili Pepper Fiesta in the fall, which bring thousands of people to the garden for crafts, workshops, and art performances.

The garden's education department also offers many programs and classes in which one can learn more about plants and how to care for them. Over 200 different horticultural courses and tours are offered every year, with certificates in horticulture, floral design, and composting given to students who complete eight courses in their chosen field. Tours, which can range as far afield as Pennsylvania in exploring wild regions and horticultural displays in the New York area, are given year-round. Both classes and tours are open to members and non-members alike; call 718-623-7220 or visit www.bbg.org for more information.

Another way to get involved is to become one of the more than 750 volunteers who help tend the garden throughout the year, giving tours, assisting at special events, and working in the garden offices and out in the garden itself. To find out about volunteer opportunities, call 718-623-7260, or fill out an on-line application at www.bbg.org.

PROSPECT PARK

N

PROSPECT PARK ZOO

FLATBUSH AVENUE

Rose Arc Pool

Beech Family

Bluebell Wood

Birch Family

Coni

Elm Family

Monocot Border

Daff

Witch Hazel Family

Rock Garden

Willow Family

Willow Family

Rose Family

Rose Family

Mi Peren Bor

Annual Border

BOTANIC GARDEN

Aster Family

Legume Family

Honeysuckle Family

Lily Pool Terrace

Warm Temperate Pavilion

Tropical Pavilion

Citrus Family

Gift Shop

Honeysuckle Family

Desert Pavilion

Terrace Cafe

Bonsai Museum

Steinhardt Conservatory

Peony and Iris Garden

Olive Family

Olive Family

Aquatic House

Butterfly Bushes

Rhododendron

Azaleas

Terminal Pond

Heath Family

Azaleas

Visitor Entrance

Discovery Garden

Children's Garden

Ho Compos Exh

Mi

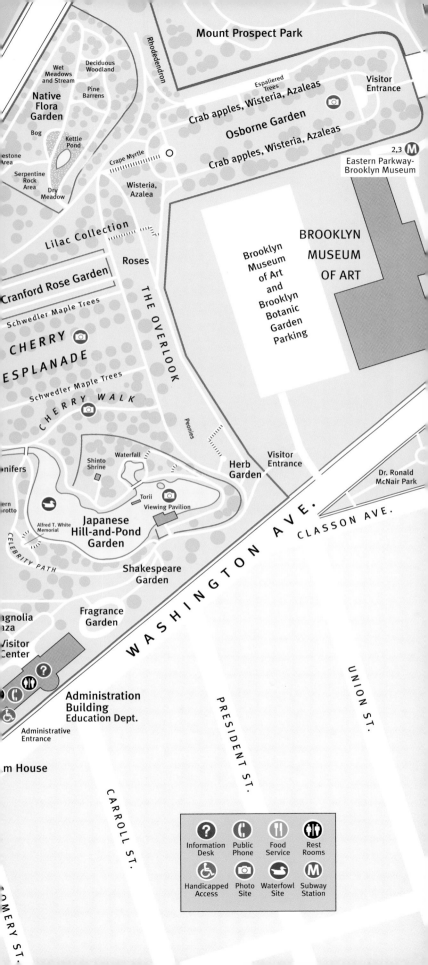

Mount Prospect Park

Native Flora Garden

Wet Meadows and Stream

Deciduous Woodland

Pine Barrens

Bog

Kettle Pond

...stone Area

Serpentine Rock Area

Dry Meadow

Crape Myrtle

Wisteria, Azalea

Espaliered Trees

Crab apples, Wisteria, Azaleas

Osborne Garden

Crab apples, Wisteria, Azaleas

Visitor Entrance

2,3 Ⓜ Eastern Parkway-Brooklyn Museum

Lilac Collection

Roses

Cranford Rose Garden

Schwedler Maple Trees

CHERRY ESPLANADE

Schwedler Maple Trees

CHERRY WALK

THE OVERLOOK

Peonies

Brooklyn Museum of Art and Brooklyn Botanic Garden Parking

BROOKLYN MUSEUM OF ART

...nifers

...ern ...rotto

Shinto Shrine

Waterfall

Torii

Viewing Pavilion

Alfred T. White Memorial

Japanese Hill-and-Pond Garden

CELEBRITY PATH

Shakespeare Garden

Herb Garden

Visitor Entrance

Dr. Ronald McNair Park

WASHINGTON AVE.

CLASSON AVE.

...agnolia ...aza

...isitor ...Center

Administration Building Education Dept.

Administrative Entrance

Fragrance Garden

...m House

UNION ST.

PRESIDENT ST.

CARROLL ST.

...OMERY ST.

Ⓠ Information Desk

Ⓒ Public Phone

Ⓣ Food Service

Ⓣ Rest Rooms

♿ Handicapped Access

📷 Photo Site

Ⓦ Waterfowl Site

Ⓜ Subway Station

Just across Flatbush Avenue from Prospect Park is another oasis of nature within the city, The Brooklyn Botanic Garden. The two are separate institutions, under separate administrations. The Park is a city agency and the Garden is a nonprofit cultural institution with an independent board of trustees. But the garden and the park do share one similarity—they are two of the city's most prominent green spaces, neighbors on the Harbor Hill moraine.

However, visits to Prospect Park and the Brooklyn Botanic Garden provide very different experiences. While the park is filled with sports and picnic fields and recreational facilities, the garden's lawns are carefully manicured and meant for casual strolling. If the park is intended as a playground of nature, in many ways the Botanic Garden is a museum of nature, which can serve both as a respite from city life and a bountiful teacher of the wonders of the plant world.

The garden's curators stress the many "gardens within a garden" that make up the botanic grounds, each with its own distinctive appearance, scent, and focus. As you walk through the garden, note the different environments you pass through: the Japanese Hill-and-Pond Garden's peaceful balance and carefully trimmed tree forms; the contemplative calm of the Shakespeare Garden; the naturalistic wildernesses of the Native Flora Garden. Each is part of the larger green space, but each also conveys a unique feel and has its own lessons to teach about the plant world.

What's in a Name?

Your best guide to the garden's plants are the small labels that are attached to all but a few specimens and convey a wealth of information for those who know how to read them. Each plant is identified by its common name (which may be one of several names the plant is known by). Beneath this is the plant's botanical or Latin name, according to a system invented in the 18th century by famed Swedish botanist Carl Linnaeus, known as the Father of

The Lily Pool Terrace and Palm House— the garden's original conservatory, now used for special events—are a popular site for strollers and photographers.

Taxonomy. Linnaeus's multivolume *Systema Naturae* set out to create a grand classification scheme for all living things, in accordance with his stated goal of revealing the order inherent in God's creation.

Each species was given a two-part name made up of the genus and the species epithet. The former is reserved for larger groupings of related plants; the latter is the fundamental unit of the classification. Linnaeus's system was simplistic in some ways, being based solely on the number and arrangement of a plant's reproductive organs. Nevertheless, his basic binomial (two-name) nomenclature has become the standard for plant and animal biologists the world over.

On the bottom right corner of each label is the plant's accession number, a unique identifier that is a key to when the specimen was first planted at the garden. The first two digits represent the last two digits of the year it was acquired by the garden, while the last four indicate where it fell in the acquisition order that year—so "950023" would mean the twenty-third plant acquired in the 1995 calendar year.

History of the Garden

Even as Prospect Park became world-famous for its picnic meadows, woodlands, and ponds, the neighboring Eastside Lands, as they were called, sat mostly vacant. Various proposals were made for use of the site—an armory was suggested at one point. But the land, mostly barren acres, sat idle for decades, used as an ash dump for the parks department.

The Eastside Lands were officially dubbed Institute Park in 1902, when the Brooklyn Museum of Art opened facing Eastern Parkway at the northern end of the lands. At the same time, enthusiasm was growing for using the plot as a botanic garden. In 1909 the city approved, providing matching funds if private donors came up with the remainder. Philanthropist Alfred T. White promptly donated $25,000 to make the garden a reality.

The Brooklyn Botanic Garden officially opened to the public on July 1, 1910 as part of the Brooklyn Institute of Arts and Sciences, which included the Brooklyn Museum and the Children's Museum. Within 4 years, the garden had expanded to 52 acres, as the city obtained the southern tip of the property, running between Malbone Street (now Empire Boulevard) and the old Flatbush town line, in 1914.

The garden's original design was laid out by the Olmsted Brothers firm, led by Frederick Law Olmsted's sons Frederick, Jr. and John Charles. Most of today's garden, though, is the work of Harold Caparn, the garden's landscape architect from 1912 to 1945, who introduced such elements as Magnolia Plaza and the Rose Garden. Unlike many previous botanic gardens, which had been laid out according to strict taxonomic principles, Caparn meant the Brooklyn Botanic Garden to be both aesthetic and instructive: a natural setting and a living museum of nature all at once. The purpose was unique: display plants in beautiful settings, teach children and adults about plants, and conduct scientific research.

Caparn's designs have mostly stood the test of time, though they have been added to and modified over the years. In the 1970s, the Brooklyn Botanic Garden was spun off from the Brooklyn Institute of Arts and Sciences, becoming its own separate organization. The Institute now consists of one remaining institution, the Brooklyn Museum of Art.

The Garden Entrances

There are three entrances to the Brooklyn Botanic Garden, one at each of the main access points of the narrow, irregular slice of land that it occupies. The entrances on Eastern Parkway and at Empire Boulevard and Flatbush Avenue are the most convenient by subway (the Eastern Parkway-Brooklyn Museum stop on the 2 and 3 train and the Prospect Park station on the D, Q, and S, respectively). The Washington Avenue entrance, behind the Brooklyn Museum of Art, is most convenient to visitors coming by car and parking is available in the museum's spacious lot.

The largest and most used entrance is on Eastern Parkway, at the head of a narrow strip of land between the Brooklyn Museum of Art and Prospect Park. A metal gate, installed in 1946, bears plaques depicting the three great cereal grains cultivated by humans—wheat, maize, and rice—while vertical panels depict in impressionistic form the evolution of plant life throughout history, from

The Osborne Garden bursts into color in springtime, as flowering crab apples, wisteria, and azaleas blossom.
At right, the centerpiece planter hosts a seasonal display of plants and flowers in a decorative stone basin.

ferns to flowering plants.

Within the entry gate, visitors pass beneath overhanging branches of a monarch birch, with dramatically striped papery bark. The path here is flanked by a pair of boulders that came from the Palisades, between Hoboken and Englewood, New Jersey. The boulders are a record of the glacier that built all of Brooklyn.

Osborne Garden

Upon entering the Brooklyn Botanic Garden from its Eastern Parkway entrance, the first space you encounter is the Osborne Garden, a formal garden utilizing the principles of Italian landscape gardening. Stone, water, and greenery produce an oasis of cool and calm in the midst of the city.

At the north end of the garden are two 35-foot-high fluted columns, their carved ginkgo leaves meant to symbolize the peace and beauty of the plant world. The stone basin between them was once used as a reflecting pool but now serves as an annual flower bed.

In spring, the Osborne Garden is a wonderland of color, beginning with the large white and pink blooms of flowering crab apples underplanted

The wisteria arbors in the Osborne Garden bring forth their lush blooms in April, bringing not just color but their rich scent to the garden.

with red, pink and fuchsia azaleas. Ten pergolas draped with climbing Japanese wisteria frame the whole scene, creating a mosaic of pinks, reds, and purples.

Since the Osborne Garden is meant to be a formal space, sitting is not allowed on the central lawn, though it's fine to walk on it.

At this garden's southern end is a stone fountain, its bowl carved from a single piece of Indiana limestone. The fountain sits within a semicircle of limestone benches with curious acoustic properties. Sit at either end, and you can whisper clearly to someone sitting at the opposite end; or, if you prefer, you can eavesdrop on them. ("Whispering chairs" such as these first attained popularity in Elizabethan England.)

Pass through twin columns at the south end of the Osborne Garden (replicas of those in Florence, Italy's, famed Boboli Gardens,) beneath a grove of European hornbeams, down a broad flight of steps and the main grounds of the Botanic Garden are spread out before you.

Louisa Clark Spencer Lilac Collection

At the foot of the stairs leading from the Osborne Garden lies the Louisa Clark Spencer Lilac Collection, named for the chairman of the board of the garden from 1977-82. Here 150 lilac bushes burst into bloom each spring with a profusion of cones of tiny flowers in a rainbow of pastel colors. Each bush blooms for about 2 weeks, with the different

varieties spanning a 6-week period in the spring and peaking around Mother's Day (the second Sunday in May), when the air is filled with their old-fashioned scent.

The garden's lilac collection contains examples of 20 of the 23 known lilac species, plus a large number of cultivars, including some of the first French hybrids, which date back to the mid-19th century. All eight known colors of lilac are represented here: white, violet, blue, pink, lilac, magenta, purple, and

The Brooklyn Botanic Garden's collection of lilacs blooms in April and May, presenting every known color of the lilac family: white, violet, blue, pink, magenta, purple, lilac, and primrose yellow. The Syringa x hyacinthiflora *'Annabel,' at lower right, is the first to bloom, in late April, with the rest of the lilacs joining it in flower by Mother's Day. The last to bloom, in mid-June, are the tree lilacs S. reticulata and S. pekinensis.*

primrose yellow, as well as a purple-and-white bicolor.

In the spring, as the lilac blossoms first appear, the ground is carpeted with purple-blue grape hyacinth blooms—an added bonus to one's visit to the collection.

Tour of the Native Flora Garden

Tucked away behind a wooden stockade fence at the garden's westernmost edge is the Native Flora Garden. With its naturalistic look and minimal labeling, this area could be mistaken for a mere woodland, especially considering the sizable trees that have grown up since it was established in 1911. But in fact, the plants here, all selected from those that thrive within 100 miles of New York City, are grown in eight distinct habitats: serpentine rock, dry meadow, kettle pond, bog, pine barrens, wet meadow and stream, deciduous woodland, and limestone ledge. Each habitat is carefully maintained with the soil and environmental conditions necessary for its particular ecology. (This area is also a showcase of the ongoing research at the garden to inventory all plants growing in the New York metropolitan area).

Serpentine Rock Formation

The small serpentine barren to the left of the entrance is one of the rarest ecosystems in the world, which, in our area, is found primarily on Staten Island and in a handful of outlying areas in New York and New Jersey. Only a few plants that are adapted to this environment can survive in it and include sumac and sassafras, and a variety of ferns.

Dry Meadow and Kettle Pond

Across the path, on the right, is the dry meadow, containing a variety of grasses and wildflowers, including those like bee balm and butterfly

weed that attract a variety of insects. Next to the meadow is a recreated kettle pond, showing how these glacier-spawned pools once looked after their creation. The ferns, the broad-leaved arrowhead, and blue flag iris are much the same as the plant cover in Prospect Park's restored Upper Pool, once a natural kettle pond.

Bog

Beyond the kettle pond and to the left is a re-created bog, an accumulation of plants that, because of the acid and anaerobic soil, fail to fully decompose, leaving the spongy humus-rich soil known as peat. Lime green or reddish mounds of sphagnum moss abound in this habitat. These plants have evolved to further acidify the soil in order to create an environment that is unfavorable for other plants. A few flowering plants such as acid-loving plants as well as insect-eating plants such as round-leaf and threadleaf sundews, however, have adapted to living in the extremely acidic conditions. Cranberries also grow here, as in the thousands of bogs across New England where they are harvested.

Limestone Ledge

To the left of the bog is a limestone ledge, typical of those that might be found in the Catskill or Berkshire mountains. Limestone is a sedimentary rock formed when calcium-rich marine organisms settle to the ocean floor. It is chiefly made of the mineral calcite, creating a soil that is as alkaline as peat bogs are acidic, and providing for just as distinctive a variety of plants. Bladdernut is planted along the top of the ledge, accompanied by wild ginger, wild geranium, and sweet wild violet, all of which thrive in the rich woodland soil.

Pine Barrens

Back on the main path, beside the kettle pond, is an example of the pine barrens that still cover large areas of eastern Long Island and southern New Jersey. Dubbed barrens because their sandy soil was unusable for farming, they support a distinct set of plant life, most notably the pitch pines that benefit from periodic forest fires. Other plants native to the barrens

Located just north of the Native Flora Garden and sheltered by tall shade-giving trees is a less frequented area of the garden where a variety of rhododendrons grow. While azaleas are members of the genus Rhododendron, *in common usage the term rhododendron refers to the plants with larger, leathery leaves, while azalea refers to those with smaller, thinner leaves. The genus* Rhododendron *is a member of the heath family* (Ericaceae) *which includes the heaths and heathers, blueberries, mountain laurels,* Pernettya, Andromeda, *and several other ornamental plant groups. Most members of this family require a rather acid soil and good drainage. More than 850 species have been described within the genus* Rhododendron.

are the scrub oak, American holly, and huckleberries and blueberries, which offer both food and protection for the animals inhabiting the barrens.

Wet Meadow
Opposite the barrens, uphill of the bog, is the wet meadow. It contains a variety of flowering plants, sedges, grasses, and rushes that grow beside an artificial stream. Jewelweed as well as turtlehead predominate and skunk cabbage, which emits an unpleasant odor, grows here in the spring.

Deciduous Woodland
The entire back section of the Native Flora Garden is given over to deciduous woodland, the forest common to this region, featuring oaks, maples, hickories, walnuts, and beeches. Among the most notable trees are a towering sweet gum planted in 1912 by Hugo de Vries, the famed evolutionary theorist and director of Amsterdam's botanic gardens, and a grove of huge beeches near the stockade fence. Along the fence path, not far from the garden entrance, stands an equally notable ancient black cherry, clumps of fungus growing high on its gnarled trunk, that is believed to have predated the Botanic Garden's creation.

The combination of running water and dense foliage in the Native Flora Garden makes it an oasis for birds, and it's an excellent locale in which to find hummingbirds and migratory songbirds in both spring and fall. The Native Flora Garden is closed from November to April, since its dirt paths would be difficult to negotiate in winter.

Cranford Rose Garden
The Cranford Rose Garden—named for subway engineer and garden patron Walter Cranford, who donated the entire $15,000 cost of its initial construction—has been one of the Botanic Garden's most popular attractions since it first opened in 1928. In June, when the roses are in full bloom, the air is filled with the sight and scent of thousands of roses. Though most are planted in labeled beds separated by paths to allow visitors easy access, others climb trellis arches or twine around concrete posts and wooden fences.

The Cranford Rose Garden contains more than 5000 bushes of nearly 1200 varieties of roses, in addition to clematises such as the one pictured below. The statue, officially named Roses of Yesterday but known around the garden as The Rose Maiden, stands bearing a sundial at the southern end of the garden.

In the Cranford Rose Garden, the rose can be seen in all its various shapes and forms. The upright hybrid teas, polyanthas, and floribundas suit the geometry of the rectangular central beds, while other types of roses with more carefree growth habits are allowed to ramble, climb, trail, and spread. In keeping with the emphasis on education at the Brooklyn Botanic Garden, each rose in the garden is labeled with its name and date of introduction. Visitors are encouraged to follow the historical development of the rose while learning about its many varieties and the best ways to grow them. They can also see that roses will flourish in any region of the United States, for here over a thousand varieties thrive in the polluted air of a city with hot and humid summers and harsh winters.

To talk of "climbing roses" is to some degree a misnomer: No roses can climb on their own, but some varieties have tall canes that can be trained to grow up and over a trellis. Clematis, above, an unrelated genus of the buttercup family, is a far more aggressive climber, making it a popular trellis garden plant.

In June and September their sweet scent attracts both human and insect visitors.

Roses have been cultivated for centuries, and known varieties number in the thousands. They fall into two broad categories. The old European garden roses are once-blooming, putting out flowers only in early summer. Modern roses, on the other hand, usually bloom repeatedly, peaking in June, and again in the fall. Almost all reblooming roses in existence today have been derived from just four original varieties of China rose. When these four plants reached Europe after 1792, they were used in breeding programs that produced many varieties of reblooming roses. These new reblooming roses quickly grew in popularity among gardeners. The well-known long-stemmed roses favored by romantics are hybrid tea roses and are a fairly recent cultivation, dating only to the 1860s.

The Cranford Rose Garden contains over 5000 bushes of nearly 1200 varieties and is the largest collection of rose cultivars in North America. The collection includes a profusion of wild species, old garden roses, hybrid teas, grandifloras, floribundas, polyanthas, hybrid perpetuals, climbers, ramblers, and miniatures. Some of the original roses planted in 1927 are still in the garden today.

The collection also includes several All-America Rose Selections (marked on their nameplates with the letters AARS and the date of their selection). AARS roses are those that have been tested throughout the country and selected for health and bloom. (The Cranford Rose Garden has been an official AARS Display Garden since the 1930s, and in 1980 was awarded the society's Public Rose Garden Award for providing public education about the cultivation and variety of roses.)

To help explain the cultivation history of roses, the Cranford Garden groups some ancestral stock with its cultivated descendants. Dates on the nameplates record when the variety was first cultivated, not necessarily when it was introduced to the Botanic Garden.

The names of the rose varieties in the Cranford Garden provide a sort of celebrity walk in themselves, with roses honoring such notables as actors George Burns and Angela Lansbury, and tennis champion Chris Evert. "Elizabeth Scholtz," a pink grandiflora introduced in 1988, is named for the garden's Director Emeritus.

Most modern rose cultivars are bred for visual appeal rather than for scent. While only the China-derived roses bloom again in the fall, all roses produce in the fall the orange and red fruits known as rose hips, which are used commercially in the production of vitamin C. The hips are especially popular with local birds, and throughout the fall and early winter one can find blue jays, cedar waxwings, and other wintering birds greedily devouring the sour rose fruits.

Cherry Walk & Esplanade

The Cherry Esplanade, for much of the year, is just a peaceful, simple lawn flanked by rows of low cherry trees. Alongside those are twinned rows of tall trees, presenting an orderly border to the quiet pastoralism of the central lawn. Adjacent to the Esplanade is Cherry Walk, a gently curving path leading to the pond in the Japanese Garden.

This Weeping Higan Cherry tree can reach a height of 30 feet at maturity, although cherries as a group tend to be short-lived unless they are well cared for.

Among the many events conducted during the two-day festival are displays of bonsai and ikebana (flower arranging), and demonstrations of sumi-e (brush painting), Japanese waterbase woodcuts, origami (paper-folding), and Japanese classical dance (below).

Taiko drumming (right) has become a high-light of the festival. It is believed to have been performed in Japan for well over 2000 years. Reputedly, one of the first uses of taiko was as a battlefield instrument; its purpose was to intimidate and scare the enemy.

Sakura Matsuri Festival

The Sakura Matsuri festival is held each spring to celebrate the flowering of the Sekiyama (Kwanzan) cherry trees that line the Cherry Esplanade.

The weekend-long festival celebrates the traditions of *hanami*, or flower-viewing, that have been developed over the centuries in Japan. There, the Japanese Meteorological Agency begins reporting the status of the cherry flowers in mid-March, following the blooms as they spread from south to north. Viewers spread *goza*, or straw mats, under the cherry trees, on which they eat delicacies and drink sake. When a breeze knocks a petal off a tree, it is placed in the sake cup. The blossoms are a symbol of *isagiyosa*, the transience of the world, and are to be celebrated without trying to hold on to their evanescent beauty.

The Brooklyn Botanic Garden's Sakura Matsuri festival has been held yearly since the early 1980s, and includes demonstrations of music, dance, and art (including bonsai) for visitors of all ages.

For a more detailed schedule, visit the garden's Cherry Watch website: www.bbg.org/visiting/virtual_garden/cherrywatch.

Cherry Walk, on the eastern edge of the Brooklyn Botanic Garden's Cherry Esplanade, provides a selection of some of the 42 varieties of Oriental flowering cherries in the garden, which make this one of the foremost cherry viewing sites outside of Japan. The different flowering times make for displays of cherry blossoms from late March to mid-May, peaking each year around the time of the annual Sakura Matsuri festival at the end of April.

Serene in off-season, all that changes in April, when the flowering cherries burst forth into a profusion of color that becomes the Botanic Garden's centerpiece. The peak of the season coincides with Sakura Matsuri, the garden's cherry blossom festival, which since 1982 has been an annual crowd-pleaser (See sidebar, page 120.) The cherry blooms fade by May, then leave the Esplanade to its off-season role as a pleasant place for strolling, photographing, or sitting—the only place in the entire Botanic Garden, in fact, where sitting on the lawns is permitted.

Herb Garden

Built partly by Works Progress Administration laborers in the 1930s, the Herb Garden is a pleasant enclave near the Botanic Garden's Washington Avenue entrance. Some of the original plants were selected by a survey of the day's top pharmacists, physicians, and surgeons; the more than 300 plants in the present collection are now selected by the herb garden curator.

In botanical terms, herbs are any nonwoody plants, but in common usage the word is applied to many other plants as well. "If you pull dictionaries off the shelf, you'll get a number of different definitions," says the garden's curator. "The word seems to cover groups of plants that seem on the surface not to have very much in common—chiefly medicinal plants, which may be either edible or deadly poisonous or anything in between, and, on the other hand, culinary herbs, which are used to flavor food but are not a chief source of calories." The Herb Garden is open to any plants useful to people, mostly as medicines or flavorings, but also for such diverse uses as cosmetics, oils, dyes, or even insect repellents.

These herb beds surround two

The Herb Garden presents a variety of plants used by humans as foodstuffs, medicines, fragrances, and dozens of other uses. Tampala (Amaranthus tricolor), at near right, is grown in Asia as a green vegetable, while its relative Amaranthus caudatus (love-lies-bleeding, or tassel flower, at far right) is cultivated in India as both a cereal grain and a green.

knot-shaped hedges, of the kind that were frequently planted in Elizabethan herb and vegetable gardens. Made of boxwood and Japanese barberry, the knot garden was installed in 1938, inspired by a design originally created in 1577 by Thomas Hill (Dydymus Montane) in Sir Frank Crisp's *Mediaeval Gardens*. The eastern half is patterned after the original, while the western half is a modern design.

The seven newly replanted beds in the Herb Garden are currently divided by uses: fragrances and cosmetics in the north central bed; oils, fibers, and dyes in the south central; plants that are drunk, smoked, or chewed to the southeast; culinary herbs and other edible plants to the northwest and southwest; and medicinal herbs along the east and north borders. The final bed to the northeast, dubbed plant curiosities, contains miscellaneous herbs that don't fit any of the other categories.

Unlike other areas of the garden, where plants are not always thoroughly annotated, here the labels describe the uses to which the herbs have been put. Among these are such traditional medicinal herbs as feverfew, cowslip, and black cohosh. Modern medicines are derived from foxglove, a poisonous plant that nevertheless provides the raw materials for the heart medicine digitalis, as well as yams, which are used in the making of synthetic estrogens and progesterone. Saint John's-wort and echinacea are represented here, too, as well as a towering ginkgo tree, source of the now trendy memory enhancer ginkgo biloba.

Common culinary plants can include peppers and eggplants, strawberries, huckleberries, and bananas, as well as such common flavoring herbs as oregano, ginger, rosemary, cardamom, and the huge-leaved turmeric plants, the underground stems of which are made into the bright yellow spice.

Herbs here that have multiple uses include fennel (grown as a vegetable and a flavoring, and also hung over the doors on Midsummer's Eve to ward off evil spirits); lavender (used in perfume and to cure headaches); mint (used as a flavoring and a source of menthol); rosemary (traditionally used to repel moths and combat "weakness of the brain," as well as for flavoring); and thyme, which in addition to being a common culinary herb produces a volatile oil containing thymol, which is used as an antiseptic, deodorant, anesthetic, and meat preserver.

The plant curiosities section has several especially peculiar specimens, including such lesser-known plants as sweet herb, which contains a compound a thousand times sweeter than table sugar and was used by the Aztecs as a sweetener. In the same bed, alongside the huge reddish blossoms of love-lies-bleeding, or tassel flower, is the mimosa, or "sensitive plant," which folds up its

leaves when touched. Here also are the tufted fronds of papyrus, looking less like a real-life plant than a Dr. Seuss creation. Its fibers provided early Middle Eastern civilizations with everything from paper to boats. The thick papyrus groves of the Nile were the bullrushes described in the Biblical tale of Moses.

The Herb Garden is best visited in summer and early fall, when the plants here have grown to their full size. Leave some time for a leisurely stroll among the herb beds, reading the labels and stories of the many ways that herbs have contributed to our lives.

Shakespeare Garden

First instituted in the 1920s, during the Shakespearean craze that was then gripping the nation, the Shakespeare Garden is devoted to plants mentioned in Shakespeare's plays and sonnets. Its original sponsor, Henry C. Folger, was also founder of the Folger Shakespeare Library in Washington, D.C.

Rather than a pure tribute to the Bard, however, it has developed into an interpretation of a classic English cottage garden of Shakespeare's time, with benches for quiet contemplation and plantings that include some cottage garden favorites such as nasturtiums and other New World plants that were unknown to Shakespeare but are well adapted to Brooklyn's local climate.

In Shakespeare's day, a cottage garden would typically lie in front of the house and would emphasize plants that were useful to the household, including savory vegetables and flavorings like thyme, leeks, onions, mustard, as well as "strewing herbs" that would be spread across the floor to repel insects and vermin and to freshen the air. Gardening was a major element of Elizabethan culture and found its way into many of Shakespeare's metaphors. The more than 80 plants here that are mentioned in the

The Shakespeare Garden exhibits plants that appeared in the works of the great playwright, as well as other flowers common to English cottage gardens. At right, hollyhock; below, delphinium.

The Fragrance Garden, designed to benefit visitors with limited vision but enjoyable by all, features a variety of plants chosen for their strong aromas or interesting textures.

works of Shakespeare are specifically noted, with nameplates containing appropriate quotations.

The Shakespeare Garden was originally located adjacent to the Children's Garden. By 1979, however, the plants had become shaded out by the large Austrian pines that had grown up alongside it, and the garden was relocated to its present site, which had previously been a plant nursery. In 2000, the Shakespeare Garden received a further face-lift, in part to widen paths to provide wheelchair access. One of the new additions, a boxwood topiary in the shape of a woodcock, is just beginning to take shape by the serpentine wall at the back of the garden.

Fragrance Garden

Between the Shakespeare Garden and the administration building lies the oval Fragrance Garden, designed by Alice Recknagel Ireys in 1955 as one of the nation's first garden exhibits for the blind. It has since become one of the garden's most popular sections, particularly with the wheelchair-bound, the elderly, children, or anyone who enjoys feeling plants' textures and smelling their aromas.

The planting beds are set atop a 28-inch-high wall, enabling easy touching and smelling of the plants by those in wheelchairs as well as on foot. Most of the plants bear metal identifying markers, in both standard type and braille; the braille type actually contains additional information, so you might want to bring a braille-reading friend to get the full scoop. Further back from the wall, flowering plants have been planted to create a pleasant backdrop for the sighted.

The plantings are divided into four sections. Working clockwise from the entrance from the Shakespeare Garden, these are: Fragrant Flowers, Plants for Touch, Plants with Scented Leaves, and Kitchen Herbs. There is also a small fountain that provides both the burble of flowing water and a washbasin for removing the smell of the plants from one's hands. this is the only garden other than the Discovery Garden in which touching of plants is allowed.

The flowering-plant bed includes

such plants as heliotrope, with its vanilla-scented aroma, and petunias. Different flowers peak in scent at different times of day: the flowering tobacco plant, for example, produces scent only in the evening, since the moths that pollinate it are nocturnal. Some other plants here have little scent but have been selected for their bright white flowers, which are visible to some visitors with limited sight.

The plants for touch exhibit a range of textures, from the silky softness of lamb's ear to the sharp thorns of the agave—the latter of which is set back from the retaining wall to encourage visitors to read the warning sign before touching. One also finds horehound, a small plant with tiny, nubbled leaves, offering a velourlike feel.

The scented leaves section contains several plants whose smells remarkably mimic other plants. To

The "cloud pruning" of plants in the Japanese Hill-and-Pond Garden is clearly visible in this view across the garden's wooden bridge.

release their aromas, gently rub the plant's leaves, then smell your fingers. Many of these are geraniums and mints: apple-scented geranium, apricot geranium, peppermint geranium, rose geranium, Corsican mint, lavender, and the strong-smelling mint relative Indian patchouli. Lemon verbena, a South American shrub with thin, tapered leaves, is especially notable for its strong lemony scent.

There are still more mints in the kitchen-herb bed: chocolate peppermint, spearmint, large-flowered calamint. Here, too, are common kitchen herbs like chives, dill, rosemary, and sage, alongside towering stalks of fennel and sweet basil. In fall, the pineapple sage accompanies its strong scent with a profusion of bright red tubular flowers.

Japanese Hill-and-Pond Garden

Of all the attractions of the Brooklyn Botanic Garden, one stands apart as both the most popular and possibly the most intricate of the gardens within a garden. This is the Japanese

Hill-and-Pond Garden, which since its creation in 1915 has been arguably the Botanic Garden's aesthetic centerpiece.

Designed by legendary Japanese American landscape architect Takeo Shiota, this was the first Japanese-style garden to be constructed in a public garden in the United States, and remains one of its finest. The space utilizes the classical conventions of Japanese garden design—terraced hillsides and carefully trimmed foliage, all reflected in still water—with several idiosyncratic touches of Shiota's. The elements combine to create an atmosphere at once both traditional and unique.

The first thing one notices upon arriving at the garden is a shogun lantern, installed here in 1980 to mark the twentieth anniversary of New York's sister-city relationship

Above, a view back across the pond toward the viewing pavilion of the Japanese Hill-and-Pond Garden. In the foreground, the snow-scene lantern rests atop Turtle Island, where its namesake amphibians surface to bask in the sunshine. At left, the 350-year-old lantern that marks the garden's entrance, honoring the memory of a 17th-century shogun.

with Tokyo, a gift from Bunjiro Sakuma, a Tokyo civil servant. The 10-foot-high stone lantern was dedicated in 1652 to honor shogun Tokugawa Iemitsu. According to lore, it was originally installed with its inscription facing away from visitors because the shogun to whom it was dedicated had fallen out of favor in 17th-century Japan.

Just inside the entrance to the garden, one steps into the viewing pavilion, a wooden-roofed structure that extends over the pond, with an attached wisteria arbor projecting from one

A Tour of the Japanese Hill-and-Pond Garden

The tour begins at the large stone lantern (1) that marks the main entry to the Japanese Garden. The 10-foot, 3-ton, 350-year-old lantern was given to New York in 1980 by Tokyo, its sister city. Just inside the garden is the viewing pavilion (2), from which you have a splendid panoramic view of the pond and a series of high hills or constructed "mountains." The circular window *(en-so)* with bamboo latticework is an element found in some Japanese homes, usually fitted with a square paper screen onto which the shadows of nearby trees are cast.

The Japanese Garden covers an area of about 3-1/2 acres, including the 1-1/2-acre pond. The large wooden structure in the pond is a torii (3), which signifies the presence of a shrine, tucked away in the pine grove on the hill beyond. This cypresswood torii is painted a bright red-orange, a color associated with Buddhism; it is modeled after the camphorwood torii that stands in the sea at Miyajima. The inscription on the torii reads *Dai-myo-jin*, which means "Great Illuminating Deity" or "Spirit of Light."

This self-guided tour follows the lower path, which is wheelchair accessible. Along the edge of the pond, you will pass plantings of Japanese irises and tree peonies (4).

You will reach the waiting bench (5), a comfortable spot to rest and enjoy a different vantage of the garden and viewing pavilion. From here, you also have a good view of Turtle Island (6), named for the turtles that bask in the sun along the rocky shore. The bridge leading to the island is called the drum bridge *(taiko-bashi)* (7) because its high, rounded shape and reflection in the water form a circle reminiscent of a taiko, or large Japanese barrel drum. On the island is the snow-scene lantern *(yukimi-doro)* (8) made of mikage granite. Its legs and broad cap or roof designed to catch the snow are characteristic of this lantern style.

On the upper path you will see a tall, stone Kasuga-shape lantern (9), another classic lantern style.

1. stone lantern
2. viewing pavilion
3. torii
4. Japanese irises and tree peonies
5. waiting bench
6. Turtle Island
7. drum bridge
8. snow-scene lantern
9. stone Kasuga-shape lantern
10. two bronze cranes
11. waterfall
12. Shinto shrine
13. white pines
14. stone bridge
15. Celebrity Path
16. Alfred T. White Memorial

Imported from Japan in 1914, it is elaborately carved with the animals from the Chinese zodiac: rat, bull, tiger, rabbit, dragon, snake, horse, lamb, monkey, rooster, dog, and wild boar.

On the wooden bridge that crosses the stream flowing from the waterfall to the pond, you have another view of Turtle Island with its lantern, rocky beach, and irregularly arranged stepping-stones. The two bronze cranes (10) at the water's edge are recastings of those that were in the Japanese garden the day it opened.

From the bridge there is also a lovely view of the waterfall (11). In a Japanese garden, a waterfall symbolizes constant change, and the sound of moving water is an important design element. This waterfall includes a deep ravine, four cascades, and large echo caverns that magnify the sound of the falling water.

After crossing the bridge, proceed up the path a short way to the path leading to the wooden Shinto

shrine (12). The shrine is dedicated to Inari, the Shinto god of harvest, and the two stone foxes on either side of the entrance gate represent messengers of the deity. The present structure was erected in 1960, replacing the original shrine. It is built of white cedar, ash, redwood, and cypress, and uses pins instead of nails. The shrine is situated in a tranquil grove of white pines (sho-rin) (13). In Japanese gardens, pines symbolize longevity.

Follow the path along the shore through the West Gate. Continue over the stone bridge (14). After crossing the bridge, you can proceed to Celebrity Path (15) to the right, or you can take the left path, which traces the south shore of the pond. Two sets of steps lead from the path up to the Alfred T. White Memorial (16), named in honor of the Japanese Hill-and-Pond Garden's original benefactor. If you continue along the lower path, you will end up back at the main entrance to the garden.

side. The entrance is low, forcing visitors (tall visitors, at least) to bow as they enter, then to raise their heads and see the garden's panorama before them.

The centerpiece is the pond, a man-made pool created on the site of an old kettle pond left by the retreating glacier, and now occupied by swarms of koi (carp) and a perpetual flock of mallard ducks, disturbing the calm surface as they splash in for landings. Looking out across the pond, one's gaze is focused on a small bridge surrounded by carefully trimmed trees and shrubs. This "cloud pruning" is meant to replicate the shapes of nature, the clouds and hills that are the backdrop to the artificial landscape of the garden.

To the right of the bridge is a granite snow-scene lantern, with broad legs and a wide roof designed to catch the snow in wintertime. The lantern rests upon Turtle Island, named affectionately for the shelled reptiles that cluster to sun themselves on its shores. Beside Turtle Island, bronze cranes stand in the shallow water at the pond's edge, replicas of originals that have been

The Celebrity Path honors famous Brooklyn residents and natives with engraved paving stones.

removed. To the left, standing in the pond, is the torii gate, marking the location of the Shinto shrine beyond. For years, this gate was a vermilion red, but it has recently been painted a traditional, if a bit garish, orange as part of the garden's restoration.

The overall composition is meant to soothe and relax, but the "nature" on display here is as symbolic as it is pastoral: some trees mimic hills and clouds, others are trimmed to appear windswept. The balance between artificial and natural is central to a Japanese garden, as is that between

change and constancy: For instance, the garden is monochromatically green for most of the year, with only the brief appearance of cherry flowers in the spring speaking to the evanescence of life.

This is meant as a "stroll garden," and paths along the water and into the hills beyond give changing perspectives on the vistas herein. Along the path that leads through the back of the garden is the shrine, dedicated to Inari, the Shinto god of harvest. Stone foxes, representing messengers of the deity, mark the entrance. The original shrine, designed by Shiota, was reconstructed by garden workers in the 1960s.

Further back along the path from the Shinto shrine, past the splashing cascade (while a loud waterfall was a Shiota innovation rather than a traditional garden element, moving water representing eternal change is standard Japanese design), is the Kasuga-shape lantern. This 350-year-old lantern, imported in 1914 from Japan, is carved with the animals of the Chinese zodiac.

The Japanese Garden recently received a $3.2 million renovation, made complicated by the fact that Shiota left no written notes of his designs. (Shiota died in 1943 in an internment camp in South Carolina, where he had been forcibly relocated along with other Japanese Americans during World War II.)

The original shoreline was restored and stone retaining walls put in place, while the rotting wood of the torii gate was reinforced with fiberglass cores. The effect is a bit austere at first, but as nature restores some of the controlled wildness of the garden to complement the artificial elements, the Japanese Garden will continue to be restored to Shiota's vision of harmony.

Celebrity Path

In 1985, the garden added an element that's more Brooklyn than botanic: Celebrity Path, a flagstone walk celebrating about 100 artists, poets, performers, and athletes who were born or flourished in Brooklyn.

Each celebrity has an 18- by 24-inch concrete paver embedded with his or her name and a stylized leaf outline cast in bronze. The names run from the famous (actors Jackie

The cultivar "Elizabeth" magnolia in bloom. Among the oldest flowering plants on earth, the yellow blossoms are another of the garden's many springtime attractions.

Gleason and Mary Tyler Moore, both of whom attended their own inductions), to the near famous (character actors Abe Vigoda and Vincent Gardenia) to the not so famous (artists George Tooker and Beverly Pepper). One of the least-known names belongs to one of the best-known inductees. Joseph Papp, the founder of the renowned Public Theater and the popular Shakespeare in the Park series, had his stone changed to his birth name of Joseph Papirofsky at his request. Each year, a committee of officials from the borough president's office decide on new inductees, with the new stones being unveiled at the annual Welcome Back to Brooklyn day each June.

The Celebrity Path meanders up the hill just south of the Japanese Garden through the garden's conifer collection and encircles the Alfred T. White memorial and amphitheater that overlooks the pond.

Magnolia Plaza

This placid, quiet area is transformed every spring by the blossoms of dozens of magnolia trees of every variety and shade, from creamy white and rich purple to pink and yellow. The earliest to bloom are the star magnolias in March, with their large white flowers; the last, the sweet-bay magnolia, with sweetly-scented creamy white blossoms, remains in flower into June. The cultivar "Elizabeth," spreading its unusual yellow flowers over the plaza's northwest corner, is a hybrid developed by the Brooklyn Botanic Garden in 1956, and named for garden donor Elizabeth Van Brunt during Queen Elizabeth II's Jubilee in 1977. An additional Elizabeth magnolia can be found near the north end of the Osborne garden.

At the center of Magnolia Plaza stands a compass and armillary sphere, which can be used to tell time by those in the know. A thin bronze rod, or gnomon, passes through the exact center of the sphere; its shadow, traveling along the interior of the sphere, traces out the time of day, though the sphere's accuracy can vary significantly according to the time of year. A guide to recalibrating the sphere according to the month is inscribed on its base, but it's generally quicker to walk to the nearby Visitor Center in the Administration Building and check the clock there.

Magnolias are among the oldest flowering plants on earth, having evolved their large-petaled flowers, it is believed, specifically to attract the beetles that were once the primary insect pollinators. Magnolia Plaza has been devoted entirely to members of the magnolia family, aside from the euonymus and privet hedges and ivy ground cover.

⊛ Tour of the Plant Family Collection

Most of the "gardens within a garden" at the Brooklyn Botanic Garden are clearly self-contained, a plot of land set aside with a specific purpose. But many visitors may not realize that much of the larger garden makes up a garden itself: the Plant Family Collection. One of the first areas to be designed by original garden architect Harold Caparn, it was intended to represent no less than the entirety of plant evolution, from the earliest land dwellers to the most recent evolutionary branches. And though new scientific discoveries since 1912 have rendered some of the original order obsolete, the Plant Family Collection still provides an excellent introduction to the many different families of plants, and gives an overview of their constituent species.

The Plant Family Collection begins on the south side of the Japanese Garden, near the feeding station for the pond's ducks. The simple plants on either side of the path here are descendants of some of the oldest land plants on earth: the ferns and other spore-bearing plants known as fern allies, which include horsetails, spike mosses, and club mosses.

Between the path and the pond here is the horsetail family, including a patch of scouring rush, thin reeds that produce fruiting bodies that were used in colonial America to scrub pots.

Though it may be hard to believe while looking at a diminutive lycopodium, 300 million years ago, during the Carboniferous Period, giant treelike club mosses covered the earth. (For comparison, reconstructed fossil fragments of a prehistoric club moss are on display in the Trail of Evolution in the Steinhardt Conservatory.) Adapted perfectly to life in wet, swampy areas, these early spore producers were eventually supplanted by seed-bearing plants, which could propagate and grow far from water; today, club mosses survive only as tiny specimens such as those on display here.

Conifers

The first of the seed-bearing plants to appear on earth were the conifers, or cone-bearing plants. With fruits still in the distant evolutionary future, conifers instead produced their bare seeds in hard, woody cones, as their descendants, from pines to spruces to firs, continue to do to this day. Over 300 different

A row of tall conifers, including redwood and cedar, make an impressive wall near the north end of the Plant Family Collection. Part of the dwarf conifer collection is in the foreground.

types of conifers are represented in the botanic garden's collection.

Probably the best-known conifer group is the pines, which can be further subdivided into trees whose needles bundle into groups of two, three, and five. The Austrian pines that line the lakeside (and are common elsewhere throughout the garden and Prospect Park) are two-needle pines; unfortunately, this makes them susceptible to a fungus called variously *Sphaeropsis sapinae* or *Diplodia pinea,* which slowly kills the tree from the bottom up, the needles turning brown and dying. These Austrian pines are infected with the fungus, and have had their lower branches trimmed back; this is only a stopgap measure, however, and Korean pines (a five-needled pine) have been planted behind them as replacement trees for the time the Austrian pines must be cut down.

Other notable conifers on this hill include several hemlocks, once an important tree used for tanning in the New York region, but now threatened except in its northernmost habitats from an infestation of woolly adelgid, an aphidlike insect originally native to Japan. On the western hillside of the conifer collection stands a famed cedar of Lebanon. This beautiful, strong tree appears on the Lebanese flag but has been logged to near extinction in that country. Alongside it is a Giant sequoia, a tree that can grow to tremendous heights in its natural habitat in the Sierra Nevada. In a northeastern climate such as New York's, sequoias tend to top out at a more modest height, such as this one has.

Though most conifers have needles and are evergreen, a few have scalelike leaves, including some junipers and cypresses, and some shed their needles in the winter, such as the larch. Several golden larches, whose needles turn a rich golden hue in autumn, are scattered along the path that skirts the eastern edge of the Japanese Garden. Dwarf variants accompany several of the conifers, showing the normal and miniature versions side by side.

Conifer species are well represented in the dwarf conifer bed on the lawn to the southwest, where visitors can find members of six of the

Between the Rock Garden and the Empire Boulevard entrance lies the Peony and Iris Garden. In late spring or early summer, the peonies emerge as dark red shoots that bear little resemblance to the shrubs they will soon become. They mature into lush, green bushes and flower a few weeks later. While the flowers last only a week or so, the garden's early, mid-season, and late varieties can display many weeks of bloom. Above, a lush display of "Bowl of Beauty." The facing page exhibits the wide range of shape and color that make repeated visits to the Peony and Iris Garden so rewarding.

seven existing conifer families. (The seventh, the monkey puzzle tree native to the Southern Hemisphere, won't grow outdoors in New York's severe weather—it needs protection—but members can be found growing in the Steinhardt Conservatory.) Originally located south of the Lily Pool Terrace, the dwarf conifers were moved here in 1984 to make way for the new conservatory. They provide not only an overview of the wide variety of conifers but also a good resource for city gardeners looking for examples of plants that can be grown in small spaces.

Ginkgo

Following the brook downstream across a small bridge, one comes upon a large ginkgo tree at the triangle where the path splits, near the south end of Cherry Walk. Common all over the globe 200 million years ago, the ginkgo now survives only as a single species native to China. As a popular street and park tree, however, it has become familiar to those in the New World as well. Along with its distinctive fan-shaped leaf, the ginkgo is perhaps best known for the malodorous seeds the female trees produce each fall; though often erroneously called a fruit, it is in fact an

aril, a fleshy seed coat. This ginkgo is a male; atop the Overlook are several females, which in autumn litter the concrete there with their odoriferous seeds.

Beeches and Birches

Opposite the gingko to the south, tucked away beneath a group of majestic oaks, is the Bluebell Wood, a recent addition that shows the curators' creative use of the garden's limited space. A bare slope much of the year, in late April and May it bursts forth into a carpet of rich color, as 40,000 Spanish bluebells spring into bloom.

The Bluebell Wood sits amid the beech family, the first major group of the Plant Family Collection's flowering plants. At the time the garden was laid out, the beeches were thought to be among the first flowering plants to have evolved. This was according to classifications by botanists Adolph Engler and K. A. E. Prantl, whose plant taxonomy was ascendant at the time of the garden's creation. Subsequently, evidence from technological advances including electron microscopy and DNA sequencing have revealed that Engler and Prantl's classifications

have been superceded. The flowering plants here, therefore, should be taken to be simply examples of the different family groupings, not necessarily representative of any evolutionary time sequence.

This wood is split into two halves, with the birch family making up the eastern half nearer the stream. The beech family, on the western side of the Bluebell Wood, contains not just beeches but the closely related oaks. One dramatic tree is an upright European beech that is almost ginkgoesque in profile, soaring perhaps five times as high as its narrow 20-foot breadth. In a circle just south of the Bluebell Wood, garden patron Alfred T. White is memorialized with a bronze plaque affixed to a stone, at the base of, appropriately enough, a towering white oak.

Just to the south of the white oak is a perhaps even more stunning tree: a Caucasian wingnut, a relative of the walnut that shares its familiar dangling catkins. This tree's thick, gnarled trunk supports several heavy branches, including one that charges off to the east with seeming disregard for the laws of gravity, suspended in midair by only the most tenuous hold on its trunk.

A pin oak displays its striking fall foliage opposite one of several willows bordering a stream that traverses the garden.

Across the path to the north sits a Camperdown elm, a direct relative of the one in Prospect Park; this one, however, has been grafted onto a taller trunk and so can do without the hillock that enables the branches of its park cousin to clear the ground.

Return to and cross the bridge by the Camperdown elm, and notice the grove of large-leaved small trees on the left bank of the stream. These are pawpaws, an eastern American native that is a taxonomic curiosity because, among other reasons, it is one of the few dicots to sport three-petaled flowers. In late summer, the pawpaw gives forth a large, soft fruit that is reputed to taste like a mix of banana and strawberry. This one has not fruited in recent years, however, perhaps because it lacks another tree to pollinate it.

Laurels and Roses

Another interesting family in this section is the laurel, one of several plant families to have oil glands, which produce strong aromas when the leaves, twigs, or roots are crushed. Just downstream from the pawpaw is a spicebush, with its little red fruits, sitting beneath a many-trunked katsura tree beside the stream. Nearby is a sassafras, with its distinctive leaves of one, two, and three lobes, and whose roots were once collected by the bushel for the production of sassafras tea.

Across the path to the east is another large family—the rose. The rose family includes a huge variety of plants with edible fruits: apples, pears, quinces, cherries, plums, peaches, and all other stone fruits; strawberries, and finally, roses, which though known for their flow-

Elm and Pawpaw Trees

On the eastern side of the woods, nearer the stream, is the elm family, another major component of the deciduous forests of this region. No American elms survive in the Garden, all having been lost to Dutch elm disease. There is, however, a smooth-leafed elm, a Eurasian species that in many ways resembles an American elm but for its slightly smaller, smoother leaves. This tree has been tapped with a metal pipe in an attempt to treat a condition of oozing bark known as wet wood, now thought to be a natural response of the tree to an infection.

In late April and May, the Bluebell Wood bursts forth into a carpet of rich color, as 40,000 Spanish bluebells spring into bloom. The flower takes its common name from the dainty bell-like shape flowers and the prevailing color.

Stars-of-persia, an ornamental onion, is among the flowering plants in the Monocot Border. Monocots, a large, diverse grouping distinct from the dicots that make up most of the flowering plants, include grasses, palms, and orchids, among others. Corn is also a monocot and is often a surprising addition to the border for visitors exploring the garden in the late summer.

ers also produce rose hips, a bitter fruit that is used in the production of teas and of commercially produced vitamin C. Hawthorn trees, whose bright red fruits in fall look very similar to rose hips, are represented here as well.

Legumes and Citruses

To the south of the rose family are the pea, or bean, family, the legumes, another extremely diverse family incorporating everything from small perennials such as indigo to larger trees like the honey locust and the yellowwood, a native of the southeastern U.S. The pea family produces more important crops than any other plant family save for the grasses. They are even more important in combination, since many peas can be combined with cereal grains to provide a complete protein, as with lentil beans and rice.

Further south still, next to the dome of the tropical greenhouse, are the citruses, or rue family, which include several large Asian cork trees. Just to the south of the path leading up past the greenhouses is a good example of a hardy orange, an Asian citrus tree that in autumn produces a seedy fruit that tastes much like a small, bitter orange.

Following the path south, one comes upon a thicket of hollies on the right, their bright red berries and deep green, pointed leaves lending a Christmasy air to an autumn day. Next to these are a grove of horse chestnuts, a common street tree first popularized in Paris. Beyond this is a kiwi arbor, beside which are planted the tea and mallow families, including several varieties of hibiscus, and marshmallow, which gave its name to the confection originally made from its roots.

Heath and Olive Families

At the southernmost reaches of the Plant Family Collection, below the terminal pond and set among a grove of pin oaks, are members of the heath family, which includes azaleas, rhododendrons, heaths, and heathers. The heaths have fungi that live inside their roots and help them absorb nutrients from the soil. As a result, heaths and related plants can grow in very poor, sandy or acidic soil.

Turn back to the north, on the west side of the stream now, and you arrive at the olive family, another diverse family that includes not just olives themselves but lilacs, forsythia, and privets, as well as ash trees, a fine collection of which stands on the side of the path opposite the smaller olives and lilacs. Nearby are the mints, whose volatile oils provide the strong scent for a large number of culinary herbs, including mint, thyme, oregano, and marjoram.

North of here, between the stream and a large open clearing, are two examples of large trees with huge, floppy leaves. Though they may at first look like cousins, they are in fact

not closely related: the paulownia, or empress tree, is an Asian native and member of the snapdragon family, and produces purple flowers in the spring and huge clusters of large pointed nuts in autumn. To the north of the three paulownias are a pair of catalpas, an eastern U.S. native of the begonia family, with similar large leaves but long, stringy seed pods in place of the hard nuts of the paulownia.

Further upstream along the brook are the poplars and willows, members of a single united family. The poplar family boasts one of the single largest living organisms on earth, a forest of quaking aspens in Colorado that are connected at the roots, making them technically a single tree. The stunning willows here are short-lived: They grow fast and die young, and new seedlings have recently been planted along the stream edge to replace the current trees when they succumb to old age.

Finally, in a small planting bed near the Rock Garden, one arrives at a family variously known as asters, daisies, or composites. Though Engler and Prantl's classification scheme is largely outmoded, here's where they got one right: This family is indeed one of the most recent to have appeared on earth. Though they may look like ordinary flowers, each daisy or sunflower is in fact a collection of many flowers: The central bull's-eye consists of numerous tiny "disk" flowers, whereas each

large petal surrounding the central disk is in fact a single-petaled "ray" flower. By this evolutionary sleight of hand, daisies and their kin are able to cause many adjacent flowers to be pollinated by a single visiting insect.

Monocot Border

Most of the flowering plants in the Plant Family Collection are of the grouping known as dicots, which germinate with two cotyledons, or seed leaves, the embryonic leaves that help to nourish a seedling as it grows. The other major flowering plant grouping in the Plant Family Collection is the monocots, which have a single cotyledon. The two branches are believed to have diverged early in flowering plant history, perhaps as much as 100 million years ago. Dicots now far outnumber their distant cousins in diversity, with about 300 families of dicots versus only 64 of monocots.

The Plant Family Collection's monocot collection is contained within the Monocot Border, which sits a bit upstream, just past a dramatic weeping willow at the water's edge. Treelike monocots like palms and yuccas are immediately distinctive for their nonwoody trunks and stalks. Most monocots have leaves with parallel veins and almost all have three-petaled flowers. (The tiger lily and iris are among the more familiar monocot flowers.) The entire grass family are monocots, including such important grain crops as corn, wheat, and oats as well as bamboos. Other well-known members of the grouping are bananas (a pair of banana plants are here, towering above their neighbors each fall) and true yams (the sweet potato, though often called a yam in this country, is an unrelated dicot in the morning glory family). Orchids are one of the most recent monocot families to evolve and by far the largest. A single example, a Chinese ground orchid, is planted here.

Rock Garden

Unlike a traditional rock garden, which would be organized around a rocky outcrop to simulate high, mountainous terrain, the Botanic Garden's rock garden is organized around a somewhat different principle. The centerpiece here are 18 boulders, all glacial erratics, that were collected on site by original

The Rock Garden provides a pleasant setting for several varieties of smaller or dwarf plants, including those that would be found in rocky mountain regions, as well as plants that are able to grow in dry or acidic soils. A small waterfall leading to a stream and pond complete the scene.

garden director C. Stuart Gager and labeled with plaques marking the type of rock and the distance it traveled via glacier before arriving in the garden. Another six original boulders are located in other parts of the garden.

At the front of the Rock Garden, beneath a row of large pin oaks, azaleas and hellebores are planted. Behind these are the drought-tolerant plants, which include many succulents. Aquatic plants, including water lettuce, grow in and around a small stream and cascading waterfall, and a "scree" section is devoted to alpine plants, mostly dwarfs, that would be found on rocky mountaintops. Acid-loving plants such as heathers and azaleas, plus a collection of evergreens, make up the remaining planting beds. Behind it all is a wall of woodland trees, mostly pines, spruces, and maples, that serve as a backdrop to the entire collection.

Lily Pool Terrace

Between Magnolia Plaza and the Steinhardt Conservatory lies the Lily

1. Woodland
Large woody shrubs and trees (including viburnums, maples, pines, and spruces) form a verdant backdrop to the Rock Garden.

2. Acid-loving Plants
These plants require acidic soil conditions. Many belong to the Ericaceae *family, including heaths, azaleas, and rhododendrons.*

3. Dry-tolerant Plants
No rain? No problem. These plants inhabit xeriscapes, landscapes where the rainfall is only 10 to 20 inches per year. Some have adaptations like succulent leaves to store water.

4. Aquatic Plants
The pond is home to plants such as water lettuce, while the pond edges are highlighted with sedges and marsh marigolds.

5. Scree
In the wild, this group of dwarf alpine plants can be found near mountaintops, flourishing in harsh, exposed stony fields formed by erosion.

6. Evergreens
Cone-bearing plants predominate in this section, particularly the dwarf or low-growing forms of conifer such as yews, junipers, dwarf spruces and firs, and false cypresses.

7. Shade-tolerant Plants
Oaks and conifers create a protective canopy over this collection, which includes shade-lovers like rhododendrons, bulbs, hostas, anemones, and hellebores.

Pool Terrace, one of the most photographed scenes in the garden. Here water lilies, sacred lotuses and other aquatic plants sprout up from a pair of long, narrow pools that stretch the length of the adjacent glass houses. Herons and egrets are frequent visitors to the pools, perching atop the plant labels and taking no notice of the humans up on land. Their interest is more in the goldfish that fill the pools.

The water lilies here are a mix of hardy and tropical plants. The garden's curators take advantage of the temperature gradient in the 4-foot-deep pools to grow tropical and hardy species side by side. The tropicals are planted in pots just 8 inches below the surface of the water, while the more hardy specimens sit in deeper, cooler water. The tropical plants, with larger leaves, more vibrant colors, and flowers that often stand upright out of the water, must be replaced annually, while the cold-resistant hardies are more durable but less dazzling. While most of the water lilies open their blooms only at midday, and begin to close up as night falls, a few—notably the "Jennifer Rebecca" and "Trudy Slocum," both at the north end of the south pool—are night bloomers, opening only as the sun sets.

At each end of the pools, sacred lotuses stand upright out of the water, with their flowers and showy seedpods peaking in July and August. There are another four

Both hardy and tropical water lilies join with elegant sacred lotuses and other aquatic plants on Lily Pool Terrace. The more dramatic blooms belong to the tropical lilies, which have larger leaves, deeper colors, and flowers that stand up from the water. At left, a sacred lotus sends up its shoots high above the water's surface, unfurling leaves, flowers, and seedpods all at the same time. In Buddhism, the sacred lotus is symbolic of the human soul, rooted in the world of experience but rising calm above its surging waters.

Tulips make their colorful seasonal appearance along the Annual Border, on the western edge of the Lily Pool Terrace. The border has seasonal displays.

lotuses in the tiny pool at the very north end of the terrace, two of which are extremely unusual. These two, in the front of the pool, are the decendants of plants grown from seeds discovered recently in a broken piece of canoe in a Chinese river, where it is believed they had lain undisturbed for more than 3000 years.

On the eastern edge of the terrace is the Mixed Perennial Border, displaying a variety of flowering plants. Its counterpart on the western side is the Annual Border, made up of a collection of annual bloomers that changes seasonally—tulips in the spring, followed by a display of annuals, showcasing the year's All-America selections, in the summer and fall.

Steinhardt Conservatory

After 20 years of planning and construction, the Brooklyn Botanic Garden opened its Steinhardt Conservatory complex in 1988 to house the thousands of plants that require climates either warmer, wetter, or drier than that of Brooklyn.

The new conservatory was twice the size of the old (a McKim, Mead & White structure built in 1914 and now restored as the Palm House, where many locals, including singer Art Garfunkel, have held their weddings).

Trail of Evolution

The entry hall to the Conservatory is occupied by the Stephen K.-M. Tim Trail of Evolution, named for its designer, a longtime Brooklyn Botanic Garden vice president who designed it in the late 1980s. From left to right, the trail traces the history of plant evolution, beginning from the earliest beginnings of life in bacteria-rich pools (the modern replica here is somewhat reduced in authenticity by the thick layer of pennies deposited by visitors), through the development of ferns and giant club mosses (a fossil club

A Japanese maple, with its miniature star-shaped leaves, makes a classic bonsai, reproducing in miniature the forms of a full-sized tree in an artistically pleasing display.

moss stump gives a sense of these extinct giants' tremendous size) and on to the appearance of the first conifers, then the flowering plants, both monocots and dicots. Along the way, educational markers explain how plant evolution was guided by global climatic changes: 280 million years ago, as the warm, wet Carboniferous Period gave way to the drier, cooler Permian, plants developed drought-resistant needles and sturdy seed-bearing cones in response, giving rise to the conifers. Another 40 million years later an increase in global temperatures and carbon dioxide levels—possibly as the result of a comet impact or an enormous volcanic eruption that occurred in prehistoric Siberia at that time—helped lead to the Great Permian Extinction, in which fully 90 percent of earth's species vanished, leaving fungi briefly the dominant form of life on the planet.

Bonsai Museum

At the left end of the Trail of Evolution is the C. V. Starr Bonsai Museum, which houses the garden's famous collection dedicated to the ancient art form of miniaturized trees, practiced in China and Japan for more than 1000 years. This collection—focused on Japanese bonsai—is the second oldest in the U.S., preceded only by the Arnold Arboretum in Massachusetts.

About 100 of the Bonsai Museum's 600 trees are on display at any one time, with groups rotated in as they reach their peak of flowering or fall colors. Particularly spectacular are the wisterias, which flower in the

A large example of a Japanese white pine bonsai is one of the attractions in the Bonsai Museum. One 300-year-old example is generally displayed in the winter.

spring; others include lilacs, azaleas, flowering cherry, and quince. One Japanese white pine bonsai that is over 300 years old generally makes its public appearance during the winter.

Any woody plant can be grown as a bonsai (roughly translated as "a plant in a pot"), whether temperate or tropical, and both Japanese imports and domestic trees are on display here. The best specimens are those trees with small leaves and fruit, so as to complete the illusion of a normal-sized tree magically shrunk to fit on a tabletop.

Bonsai trees require an extraordinary amount of care, including repeated pruning of both branches and roots to maintain their shape and compactness, shaping with copper or aluminum wire, watering frequently, addition of fertilizer every two weeks, and constant attention to temperature and humidity. The bonsai trees in the main part of the museum are temperate, and adapted to New York's cold winters. (The temperature in this greenhouse is allowed to drop as low as 28°F in the winter months.)

Tropical plants such as oranges and guava are in the cases along the right-hand wall.

When visiting the Bonsai Museum, remember that these plants are very fragile and very old. To avoid knocking loose a 300-year-old tree limb, keep your distance from the trees as you admire the artistry of both nature and human design that went into them.

Robert W. Wilson Aquatic House

The conservatory's Aquatic House features a wide variety of aquatic plants, ranging from those that live nearly entirely submerged to humidity-loving epiphytes (tree-dwelling plants) such as orchids, whose remarkable hanging roots draw moisture directly from the air under the humid conditions of their native habitat. As the only unshaded tropical greenhouse in the garden, it is a haven for plants that thrive in bright, hot, and humid conditions.

The Aquatic House's main pool contains huge tropical Victoria water lilies, their pads nearly 4 feet

A rich variety of plants are displayed in the Robert W. Wilson Aquatic House including water lilies like the Nymphaea *cultivar* Daubeniana *(inset top) and water hyacinths (top right). Orchids are on rotating display and include such hybrid genera as* Doritaenopsis *(top right) and* Potinara *(bottom right) and the epiphytic species* Aerides odorata *(bottom left). Epiphytes, or air plants, as they are called, grow on trees rather than growing on the ground.*

At first glance, the Desert Pavilion appears sparse in comparison to its lush neighbor, the Tropical Pavilion. However, on closer inspection, a wide variety of forms and colors emerge such as the spiky Yucca carnerosana and the gray-green Encelia farinosa *(near right)*. The red and yellow blossoms of a 30-year-old Opuntia *cactus (facing page, top)* and the brilliant flowering of the Chamaecereus silvestrii *are a surprise to visitors who think that cactus only bears spines.*

across. As you circumvent the pool, you must wend your way through a jungle of dangling roots and duck past towering papyrus reeds and prayer plants with their arrow-shaped leaves and tiny purple-and-white flowers. Surrounding the main pool are "water gardens," planters with floating and submerged plants.

Orchids grow most abundantly in tropical and subtropical forests, and the conditions in the Aquatic House make it a perfect environment to display some of the more interesting species. But of the garden's approximately 2000 orchids, only about a hundred are on display here at any given time as the plants are rotated as they come into blossom. Some are suspended overhead, as they would be in their natural habitat; others are set in a separate case, for better viewing of their remarkable, colorful flowers.

The Aquatic House is also the home of the insectivorous plant collection, featuring plants such as Venus's-flytraps, sundew, and pitcher plants that can trap and digest insects for their nutrients.

The Aquatic House is currently in the midst of a significant redesign, with such plants as mangroves being added to the water lilies and other aquatic plants that have long been here. The new growth provides a wilder environment in which visitors can lose themselves. The deep pool at the north end has been redesigned as a paladarium, with a variety of submerged and shoreline plants and which replicates the range of environments in which aquatic plants can thrive.

Desert Pavilion

A home for plants from warm deserts and other arid regions of the globe, the Desert Pavilion contains representative plantings from the Americas and Africa, roughly organized according to geographic origin.

Included here are plants exhibiting what's known as convergent evolution: The tendency for unrelated species to evolve into similar forms in response to the same climatic condi-

tions, even if the two are on opposite sides of the globe. Aloe and agave, for example, look almost identical to the untrained eye, though the African aloes share no immediate genetic background with the New World agave. Likewise, the spurges native to southern Africa may look remarkably like cacti, but they are in fact just a similar adaptation to the arid climate prevalent in that region. The southern African section here also includes a glass-enclosed case displaying some of the world's oddest plants: *Lithops*, or "Living Stones," that have adapted to mimic stones in their habitat in order to deceive predators.

Tropical Pavilion

The largest of the Steinhardt Conservatory's three main greenhouses at 6000 square feet, the Tropical Pavilion provides a wide variety of economic and ornamental plants from hot, wet regions of the globe.

On entering the Tropical Pavilion, visitors are struck by the high humidity level needed to maintain the lush foliage that seems to overwhelm the space and soar to the very top of the greenhouse. But hidden within this dense forest of greenery are brilliant flashes of color as in this Justica carnea, or Brazilian plume (inset right), as it is commonly named.

Two interesting specimens in the Tropical Pavilion include (left) Pachystachys lutea *(Yellow Shrimp Plant) that forms a clump of upright stems with a "candle" of bright golden yellow bracts at the tip of each stem and (above)* Costus barbatus *(Red Tower Ginger or Spiral Ginger) popular as a cut flower since the blossom can last as long as a month on the plant.*

Since even in a greenhouse this size, there's no room for a full rain forest with a forest canopy, the Tropical Pavilion is designed to represent what might exist along the Amazon River or in clearings in tropical forests, including a large mahogany tree and many large palms. It's also where many of our houseplants came from originally, since these are plants that have evolved to survive in warm temperatures year-round.

The plants in the Tropical Pavilion are organized by usage, with four major divisions: fragrance, food, medicine, and industry, with ornamental plants scattered throughout. Working clockwise, the first section is food, including many plants that bear tropical fruits, such as bananas, breadfruits, mangoes, coffee, cocoa, tamarind, and other well-known foods and flavorings. Banana plants, a fast-growing nonwoody herbaceous plant, will grow almost to the greenhouse's 65-foot-high ceiling in just a year before bearing fruit and then dying. Here, too, is a vanilla vine—actually a variety of Central American orchid—which bears stringy vanilla beans. Vanilla beans have been hand-pollinated by humans for over a thousand years, and it's believed that the plant's natural pollinator may now be extinct.

Other plants contained in the Tropical Pavilion include the rosy periwinkle (used for medicines), industrial plants like mahogany and the rubber tree, and fragrance plants

like jasmine. A profusion of palms and cycads completes the rich thicket of growth that fills the pavilion.

Because this greenhouse must be kept warm in the winter (between 70°F and 80°F), it's a popular destination in the colder months. Pop in out of the cold and enjoy a trip to another world, one that is increasingly endangered by the logging and farming that has encroached on tropical environments.

Helen V. Mattin
Warm Temperate Pavilion

Neither tropical nor desert, the Warm Temperate Pavilion is largely devoted to plants from the sections of the globe that have what's known as Mediterranean climates—typified by warm, dry summers and cool, wet winters. In addition to the

Clivia miniata, *or Kaffir lilies, are native to South Africa. If the flowers are pollinated they produce a cherry-sized, green berry which slowly turns red over many weeks.*

The brilliant blooms of the bougainvillea—usually found in shades of brilliant red or purple—fill the Warm Temperate Pavilion in the spring. Another plant native to the pavilion's climate includes the fragrant olive, which though best known for its fruit produces strong-scented flowers as well.

Mediterranean itself, this climate is common to coastal California, the Chilean coast around Santiago, parts of South Africa, and much of western Australia.

All these regions share a distinctive look, thanks to the specific climatic conditions that affect the foliage. To survive the dry season in summer, for example, many of the plants here have developed such adaptations as silver foliage and hard, waxy leaves that work to prevent moisture loss.

Along the back wall is the Cape flora collection, containing plants native to a tiny region of western South Africa that is considered a distinct floristic region, one of only seven worldwide. The Warm Temperate Pavilion is one of the few places in the eastern U.S. where one can see the wide variety of bulbs and shrubs native to this region.

The Mediterranean climate is also that of the Fertile Crescent, the swath of land where early Middle Eastern and southern European civilizations first came to prominence. Many of the staple fruits and plants of those times are on exhibit here, including fig, bay laurel, and olives, plus such familiar herbs as rosemary and mint. Perched high up on a re-created rock outcropping to the right

The Children's Garden is used by children of all ages. Here, an Adult Education instructor illustrates principles of basic gardening using a cabbage growing in the field.

The Discovery Garden provides fun and educational experiences for children of all ages. Younger children, accompanied by their parents, are particularly taken with the multicolored flowerings during the spring and summer.

of the entrance is a cork oak, a genuine oak tree that grows throughout the Iberian peninsula, where its bark is harvested to make corks.

In midwinter, the Warm Temperate Pavilion is filled with the sweet-scented flowers of fragrant olives and oranges. (Oranges, though native to tropical southeast Asia, are cultivated throughout the Mediterranean zones.) Similar to their relatives the lilacs, the small, cream-colored fragrant olive flowers grow on a long stem arising from the leaf axils.

Children's Garden

In addition to cultivating an interest in gardening among adults, since 1914 the Brooklyn Botanic Garden has run its own Children's Garden—the first of its kind in the country. Here, children age 3 to 17 can plant their own crops and flowers and harvest them in the fall under the guidance of garden instructors. For older children, lessons in science and urban ecology accompany the gardening, and teenagers who successfully complete the program can go on to become Junior Instructors.

The gardening programs are limited to 500 children each year and are generally full to capacity. Limited scholarships for all age groups are available based on financial need. For information, call the registration office at 718-623-7220.

Discovery Garden

Alongside the Children's Garden is the smaller Discovery Garden, geared toward younger children and toddlers. The Discovery Garden includes numerous kid-size exhibits and arbors, plus a "hiding tree" where children can hide among its weeping branches.

INDEX

Page numbers in ***boldface italics*** refer to illustrations.

A

Alloy Orchestra, 75
Ambergill, 44, 55
Ambergill Falls,
    55, 55–56
Ambergill Pool, 29
American Museum of
    Natural History, 25
Animal Lifestyles
    building, 20, 90–91
Animals in Our Lives
    building, 21, 91
Annual Border, 146, ***146***
Army Group (MacMonnies),
    33, 34, ***34***, 36
athletic fields, 80, 93
Audubon Society Center
    67, 68, 70

B

Bacon, Henry, 30, 50
Baerer, Henry, 38
Bailey Fountain, 37
Bald Eagle, ***89***
Bandshell, 48, 49, 74
barbecuing, 20
    zones, 49, 78
Barnes, Demas, 73
Bartel, Emil J., Jr., 48
Bartel-Pritchard Circle, 48
baseball, 93
Battle Pass, 60–61, 62
Bazile, Deenps, 78
beeches, 138
"Behind the Fences
    Tours," 53
Belle Isle Park (Detroit), 27
benches, 28
Beton Coignet, 70, ***70***
bicycling, 92–93
Binnen Bridge, 65
Binnen Falls, 64, ***64***, 65
Binnenwater, 64
Binnen Water Pool, 64
birches, 138
birdhouses, 28
birds, 55, 75, 82, 94–97
bird-watchers, 82
blind, exhibits for, 127
Bluebell Wood, 138, ***139***
Boathouse, 22, ***66–67***,
    66–68
    view from, ***66–67***
boating, 76, 93
Swan boat, ***46***
Boboli Gardens columns
    replicas, 108–109, ***109***
bog, 113
Bonsai Museum, ***147***,
    147–148
Boulder Bridge, 56
Boy Scout Marker
    Monument, 41

Breeze Hill, 70, ***70***
Brooklyn, ***9***
    history of, 8–9
Brooklyn, Battle of, 24,
    43, 62–63
Brooklyn Botanic Garden,
    100–155
    directions to, 6–7
    entrances, 108
    guided tours, 103
    history of, 107–108
    map, 104–105
Brooklyn Center for the
    Urban Environment
    (BCUE), 22, ***45***, 46
Brooklyn Eagle, 9, 74, 75, 91
Brooklyn Institute of Arts
    and Sciences, 107
Brown, H. K., 37
Brunt, Elizabeth Van,
    133–134
Bunjiro Sakuma, 129

C

Camperdown elm, 69–70
    Botanic Garden, 139
    Prospect Park, ***68***
Caparn, Harold,
    107–108, 134
Capybara, ***88***
Carmel, Charles, 84
carousel, 42
Carousel, The, 21, 84, ***84***
Cashmore, John, 50
Celebrate Brooklyn!
    Festival, 49, 74
Celebrity Path, ***132***, 132–133
Central Park, 52
Cherry Walk & Esplanade,
    119–122, ***122***
Children's Garden, 155, ***155***
Children's Historic House
    Museum, Leffert's
    Homestead, 21, ***85***, 85–87
Children's Playground,
    original plan, 59
Christian Weekly, 30
citruses, 140
Civic Virtue fountain
    (MacMonnies), 36
Cleft Ridge Span, 70, ***70***
    view from, 66
clematis, ***117***, ***118***
Cleveland, Grover, 32
Clift, Montgomery, 83
climbing roses, ***118***
Clinton, General Henry,
    62
cloud pruning, ***128***, 132
Columbia Enthroned
    Fountain
    (MacMonnies),
    32, 36
Concert Grove, 71, ***71***

Concert Grove Pavilion.
    See Oriental Pavilion
Congo Square Drummers,
    77
conifers, 134, ***134***
Cotton-top Tamarin, ***89***
Cranford Rose Garden,
    114–116, ***114–118***
Cranford, Walter, 114
Croquet Grounds, 41
Croquet Shelter, 41
Crown Heights, 83
culinary plants, 124, 127
Culyer, John, 28, 44

D

Daily News, 72
Dairy Cottage, 56
Darlington, F. W., 37
Davis, Alexander Jackson,
    50
deciduous woodland, 114
Desert Pavilion, ***150***, 151
De Vries, Hugo, 114
Discovery Garden,
    155, ***155***
Discovery Trail, 87, 90
    map, 86
Dodgers, Brooklyn, 83
dogs, rules for, 20
Dongan, Thomas, 62
Dongan Oak, Site of the,
    60, 61
Downing, Andrew
    Jackson, 24, 26
drum bridge, 130
Drummers' Circle, 75
Drummers' Grove, 74, 77
dry meadow, 112
Duncan, John H., 32, 33, 39
Dutch elm disease, 41–42
Dutch West India
    Company, 8

E

Eakins, Thomas, 36
Eastern Parkway, 9
East Wood Arch, 84–85
Ebbets Field, 38, 83
Electric Fountain
    (Darlington), 37, ***37***
Elephant House, 56
elm trees, 139
Embury, Aymar, II, 49, 90
Emerald Tree Boa, ***91***
Endale Arch, ***57***, 57–59
Enterdale Arch.
    See Endale Arch
Esdale Bridge, 55
Estern, Neil, 37, 50
Experience of Place, The
    (Hiss), 58

F

Fallkill, 53–54, **54**
festivals
    at Botanic Garden,
        87, 103, 120–121,
        120–121, 122
    Celebrate Brooklyn!
        Festival, 49, 74
    Chili Pepper Fiesta, 103
    Harvest Fest, 87
    Linsey-Woolsey
        Weekend, 87
    Sakura Matsuri
        Festival, 120–121,
        120–121, 122
    Winter Fest, 87
fishing, 76
Flatbush Turnpike
    Tollbooth, 84–85
Folger, Henry C., 126
Ford Bridge, 78
fountains, 37
Fragrance Garden,
    127, 127–128
Free Spirit, Agnes, 77
French, Daniel Chester, 49
Friends of Prospect Park.
    See Prospect Park
    Alliance
Friends Cemetery, 83
Fulton, Robert, 8

G

Gager, C. Stuart, 143
Gallagher, John, 62
gardening,
    colonial-style, 87
garden members, 103
geology (Prospect Park),
    52-53
ginkgo, 136, 138
glacial erratics, 53, 54
Goldman, Edwin Franko,
    65, 74
Goldman, Richard Franko,
    74
Grace Hill, 50
Graff, M. M., 36, 79
Gran Bwa, 78
Grand Army Plaza, 32–40
    Memorial Arch,
    30–36, ***33***
    quadriga (MacMonnies),
    36
Grant, Ulysses S. (relief), 36
Grecian Shelter, 22
Green, Andrew Haswell,
    23, 27
"Green-A-Thon," 20
Greene, Nathanael, 62
Greensward Plan, 25, 27
Green-Wood Cemetery,
    8, 23

H

Hall, George, 8
Hamadryas baboons, **89**
Hansberry, Lorraine, 65
heath family, 140–141
Heckscher, August, 60
Helmle, Frank J., 46, 68
Helmle, Huberty, and
    Hudswell, 46
Herb Garden,
    123–125, ***124-125***
Hill, Thomas (Dydymus
    Montane), 124
Hiss, Tony, 58
Horse Tamers
    (MacMonnies),
    36, **78**, 79
horseback riding, 93
horticultural courses, 103
Horticulturist, The
    (journal), 26
Howe, General Sir
    William, 62
Huberty, Ulrich, 68

I

Iemitsu, Tokugawa, 129
Imagination playground,
    21
Ingersoll, Raymond, 83
Ireys, Alice Recknagel,
    127
Iris and Peony Garden,
    136–137
Irving, Washington
    (memorial), 73

J

Japanese classical dance,
    120
Japanese Hill-and-Pond
    Garden, 53, 106, ***128***,
    128–132, ***129***
    map, 130–131
    tour, 130–131
Jefferson Market
    Courthouse, 25
Joffre, Marshal Joseph, 49
jogging, 93

K

kettle ponds, 53, 113
Kingsley, William, 9
knot garden, 124

L

Lafayette, General Marie
    Joseph du Motier de, 49
Lafayette Monument,
    49, 49–50

Lake, 28, 71–81, **77**
"Lalla Rookh" (Moore), 59
Lancaster, Clay, 42
laurels, 139–140
lawn tennis, 44–45,
    44–45
Lefferts, Peter, 85
Lefferts Homestead
    Children's Historic
    House Museum,
    21, **85**, 85–87
legumes, 140
Lilac Collection,
    110–112, ***110–111***
Lily Pond, **64**
Lily Pool, ***144–145***
Lily Pool Terrace,
    106–107, 143–146
Lioness and Cubs, (Peters),
    91, **91**
limestone ledge, 113
Lincoln, Abraham
    relief panel of, 36
    statue of (Brown), 37, 73
Lindsay, Mayor John, 60
Linnaeus, Carl, 106–107
Litchfield, Edwin,
    47, 50
Litchfield Villa,
    22, 50, ***50–51***
Little League, 46, 93
Long Meadow East, 57–70
Long Island, Battle of.
    See Brooklyn, Battle of
Long Meadow,
    28, 39, 40, **40**, 40–50
Lookout Hill, **29**, 81–82
lotus, sacred,
    144–46, ***145***
Low, Seth, 32
Lower Pool, 46–49, **47**, 53
Luciano, Edward, 83
Lukeman, Augustus, 76
Lullwater, 65–66
Lullwater Bridge,
    66, 69, **69**

M

MacMonnies, Frederick,
    32, **34**, **35**, 36, 38,
    39, 59, **78**
Macy's catch-and-release
    fishing contest, 76
Madge, Dennis, 56
Magnolia Plaza,
    133, 133–134
Martin, C. C., 58
Maryland Monument,
    81, **82**
Mattin, Helen V., Warm
    Temperate Pavilion,
    153–155, ***154***

Maxwell, Henry (relief of), 38
McCray, Abiodun, 77
McKim, Mead & White, 30, 46, 79, 83
McLaughlin, Hugh, 47
Meadowport Arch, *39*, 39–40, 58
medicinal herbs, 124
Meerkats, *89*
Menagerie, 56
Mixed Perennial Border, 146
Model Boathouse, 76, *76*
Monocot Border, 140–141, *141–142*
Moore, Douglas Stuart (bust), 73
Moore, John, 85
Moore, Marianne, 68, 69
Moore, Thomas, 59
Morton, Will, VIII, 84
Moses, Robert, 30–31
  and Bandshell, 49
  and baseball fields, 46
  and Lioness Statue, 91
  and Oriental Pavilion, 72
  sheep banished by, *40*, 41
  and zoo, 87
Mott family, 83
Mould, Jacob Wrey, 25
Muir, John, 22
music, 74–75
Music Grove, 65
Music Pagoda, 64–65, *65*, 74
Music Pagoda Bridge, 64
Music Island, 69, 71, 73, 74, *74–75*

N

National Register of Historic Places, 22
Native Flora Garden, 106, 112–114
Navy Group (MacMonnies), 35, 36, *36*
Nellie's Lawn, 60
Nethermead, 61, 64
Nethermead Arches, *60–61*, 61
New York Daily Times, 26
New Yorker, 84
New York Philharmonic Orchestra, 75
New York Sun, 36

O

O'Donovan, William, 36
olive family, 140-141

Olmsted, Frederick, Jr., 107
Olmsted, Frederick Law, 23, 26–27, *27*, 30
  career, 26–27
  and Concert Grove, 71
  and design of Prospect Park, 27, 28, 57, 83
  and Endale Arch, 58
  and Fallkill, 54
  and Long Meadow, 40, 44
  and Lookout Hill, 82
  and Parade Grounds, 80
  partnership with Vaux, 25–26
  and the Ravine, 50–52
  Stranahan and, 9
  as supervisor of construction, 28
  and Upper Pool, 46, 55
  and Vale of Cashmere, 59
  on view from Cleft Ridge Span, 66
Olmsted, John Charles, 107
orchids, 148, *148*, 151
Oriental Pavillion, 71–72, *72–73*
Osborne Garden, *108–109*, 108–110
  Wisteria arbors, *110–111*

P

Palm House, *106–107*
Papp, Joseph, 133
Parade Grounds, *79*, 79–80
park entrances
  Bartel-Pritchard Circle, 48
  Flatbush entrance, 91
  Grand Army, 39
  Ninth Street, 49
  Willink entrance, 83–87
Parks Department, 48
  Ravine restoration, 52
Parma Wallaby, *88*
paths, 30
pawpaw trees, 139
Payne, John Howard, 43
Peninsula, 81, *80-81*
Pergola, 79
Peristyle, *78*, 79
Pickering, Arthur D., 76
Picnic House, 42–43, *42–43*
picnicking, (Prospect Park), 20
pine barrens, 113–114

Pinkster Day, 87
Plant Family Collection, 134–142
plant identification, 106–107
plants for touch exhibit, 128
playgrounds, 21
Plaza Fountain (Vaux), 37
prairie dogs, *87*, 90
Pritchard, William J., 48
Prospect Hill, 24
Prospect Hill Reservoir, 24
Prospect Park, 10–99
  creation of, 22–31
  directions to, 6–7
  geology of, 52–53
  maps, 12–19
  walking tours, 18–19
Prospect Park Alliance, 31, 50–51, 68, 69, 85
  and Camperdown elm, 70
  and Carousel, 84
  and Oriental Pavilion, 72
  and Ravine restoration, 52
Prospect Park Baseball, 93
Putnam, Israel, 62

Q

Quaker cemetery, 83
Quaker Hill, 82–83

R

Raeburn, Boyd, 48
Ravine, 29, 50–53
Reagon, Toshi, 74
Red Panda, *89*
Refectory, 81
restoration, 31
  Binnenwater, 64
  Carousel, 84
  Midwood, 57
  Music Pagoda Bridge, 64
  Oriental Pavilion, 72
  trees and, 44
  Upper Pool, 54
rhododendrons, *112–113*
Rock Garden, 53, 142–143, *142–143*
Rose Garden (Prospect Park), 59–60
  lily pond in, *59*
Rose Garden, Cranford, 114–119, *114–118*
roses, 114-119, *114–118*, 139–140

Roses of Yesterday
  (Rose Maiden) (statue),
  115
running, 93
Rustic Shelter, 39, 56, **56**

S

sacred lotus,
  144-146, **145**
St. Patrick Society, 73
Saint-Gaudens, Augustus,
  36
Sakura Matsuri Festival,
  120–121, **120–121**, 122
Sargent, Charles Sprague,
  29
Savage, Eugene, 37
scented leaves,
  plants with, 128
Schneider, Arthur, 48
sea lions, **86**, 87
serpentine rock formation,
  112
Shakespeare Garden,
  106, 125–127, **126**
sheep, **40**, 41
Shelter by Road Steps, 58
Sherman, General William
  Tecumseh, 32
Shinto shrine, 131, 132
Shiota, Takeo, 129
skating. *See* Wollman Rink
Skene, Alexander J. C.
  (bust), 38
sledding, 42
Slocum, General Henry
  Warner (statue), 38–39
Snowy Owl, **88**
softball, 93
Soldier's and Sailor's
  Memorial Arch,
  32–36, **32-33**
special events.
  See festivals
Spencer, Louisa Clark,
  Lilac Collection,
  110–112, **110–111**
sports, 80, 92–93
Stark, Abe, 37
Starr, C. V., 147
statues in Botanic Garden
  Roses of Yesterday
  (Rose Maiden), **115**
  stone lanterns,
  129, 129, 130, 132
statues in Prospect Park
  Army Group
  (MacMonnies),
  33, 34, **34**, 36
  Beethoven, Ludwig von,
  72, 73
  Grand Army Plaza
  quadriga
  (MacMonnies), **33**, 36

Grieg, Edvard, 72
Hale, Nathan, 36
Horse Tamers
  (MacMonnies),
  36, **78**, 79
Kennedy, John F., 37
Lincoln, Abraham,
  (Brown), 37, 73
Lioness and Cubs,
  (Peters), 91, **91**
Moore, Douglas Stuart,
  73
Mozart, Wolfgang
  Amadeus, **73**
Navy Group
  (MacMonnies),
  35, **35**, 36
Skene, Alexander J. C.,
  38
Slocum, Henry Warner
  (MacMonnies), 38
Stranahan, James
  (MacMonnies), 36
von Weber, Anton
  Friedrich Wilhelm, 72
Warren, General
  Gouverneur Kemble
  (Baerer), 38, **38**
Steinhardt Conservatory,
  146
Stiles, William, 25
Stirling, General William
  Alexander, 62
stone lanterns,
  129, 129, 130, 132
  shogun lantern, **129**
Stranahan, James,
  8, 9, 23, **23**, 24, 47
  statue, 36
Sullivan, John, 43, 62
Sullivan Hill, 43, 44
Swan Boat Lake.
  See Upper Pool
Swartwout, Edgerton, 37
Szold, Henrietta, 43

T

Taiko drumming, **120–121**
tennis, 93
  lawn 44–45, **44–45**
Tennis House,
  43, 44–46, **45**
Terrace Bridge, 70–71
Terrace Cafe, 102
Thaw, Harry, 49
Thirteenth Regiment
  Band, 74
Thomas, Tupper, 31
Tim, Stephen K.-M., 146
Trail of Evolution,
  146–147
Tree Nymph Frog, **88**

trees, 98–99.
  See also Plant Family
  Collection
  American chestnut, 98
  blight, 98
  American elm, 98-99
  beeches, 99, 138
  birches, 99, 138
  cherries,
  119, **119**, 121, 122,
  122-123
  Black, 98
  Sekigawa
  (Kwanzan), 121
  Weeping Higan, **119**
  Camperdown elm,
  68, 69–70, 139
  conifers, 134, **134**
  elm, 139
  ginkgo, 136, 138
  hawthorns, 99
  linden, 99
  maples, 99
  near Falkill pool, 54
  near Upper Pool, 54–55
  oaks, 98
  on the Long Meadow,
  43, 43–44
  originally planted in
  Prospect Park, 28
  pin oak, **138–139**
  sassafras, 99
  sour gum, 98
  sweet gum, 98
  tree moving machine,
  28, **28**, 44
  tulip tree, 99
  walnuts, Black, 99
  Weeping Higan Cherry
  tree, **119**
  willow, **138–139**
  on western perimeter
  of lake, 48
Tropical Pavilion,
  151, 152, 153, **153**
tulips, 146, **146**
Turnpike Tollbooth,
  84–85
Turtle Island, 130, 132

U

United German Singers
  of Brooklyn, 73
Upper Pool, 46–49, **47**,
  53, 54–55

V

Vale of Cashmere,
  53, **58**, 59
Valley Grove Bridge, 56
Valley Grove House, 60

Vaux, Calvert,
23, 24–25, *25*, 27, 30
career, 24–25
and Concert Grove, 71
and design of Prospect
Park, 32, 57, 71,
82, 83
and Fallkill, 54
and Long Meadow, 40
and Parade Grounds, 80
partnership with
Olmsted, 25–26
and the Ravine, 50
Stranahan and, 9
and Terrace Bridge,
70–71
and Upper Pool, 46, 55
Villages and Cottages, 24
Viele, Egbert, 24, 80
viewing pavilion, 129, 132
Villages and Cottages (Vaux),
24
volunteers, 103
von Weber, Anton
Friedrich Wilhelm (bust),
72

W

*Walks and Talks of an
American Farmer in
England* (Olmsted), 26
Warren, General
Gouverneur Kemble
(statue), 38, *38*
Washington, George, 62
water, 50–51
water lilies,
144, *145*, 148,
148, 151
weirs (Ambergill), 57
Wellhouse, 80–81
West Drive, 48
West Woods, 44
wet meadow, 114
White, Alfred T., 107
Memorial, 131, 133
White, Stanford,
38, 39, 48, 78
wildlife, 75–76, 82, 94,
94–97
Upper Pool, 54–55
wildlife center, 87–91
Wildlife Conservation
Society, 90
Willink Information
Center, 85

Wilson, Robert W.,
Aquatic House,
148–149, *148–149*, 151
Windsor Terrace, 48
Wisconsin ice sheet
(glacier), 26, 52, *53*, 58
Wollman Rink, 30, 73, 75
Works Progress
Administration
and Herb Garden, 123
and wildlife center, 87
World of Animals
building, 20, 90
World War I Honor Roll,
49, 76

Z

Zimmerman, Christian, 58
Zoo, Prospect Park,
20–21, 86–91
animals, 86-91, *86–91*
Discovery Trail, 86–87
map *86*
Moses, Robert, and,
31, 91